Was she pretty?

Was she pretty?

LEANNE SHAPTON

DRAWN + QUARTERLY

drawnandquarterly.com

First Drawn & Quarterly edition: February 2016.
10 9 8 7 6 5 4 3 2 1. Printed in China.

Library and Archives Canada Cataloguing in Publication:
Shapton, Leanne, author, illustrator; *Was She Pretty?*/
Leanne Shapton. Originally published: New York: Sarah
Crichton Books/Farrar, Straus and Giroux, 2006. ISBN
978-1-77046-227-4 (paperback). 1. Graphic novels. I. Title.
PN6733.S485W37 2016   741.5'971   C2015-904932-6

Published in the United States by Drawn & Quarterly, a client
publisher of Farrar, Straus & Giroux. Orders: 888.330.8477.
Published in Canada by Drawn & Quarterly, a client publisher of Raincoast Books. Orders: 800.663.5714.

Canadä̈   Drawn & Quarterly reconnaît l'appui
du gouvernement du Canada/Drawn &
Quarterly acknowledges the support of the Government
of Canada and the Canada Council for the Arts for our
publishing program.

FOR
KRISTIN
DEIRDRE
SARA
ANNE
MARY
KIM
AND BOTH
CHRISTINES

CONTENTS

Was she pretty?

IN NORSE MYTHOLOGY, FENRIS,
A GREAT WOLF, WAS CHAINED
UNTIL RAGNAROK — THE
FINAL DESTRUCTION OF
THE WORLD.

THE THINGS THAT MADE
UP THE CHAIN THAT BOUND
THE FENRIS WOLF WERE
"ALTOGETHER UNKNOWN."

What is it
that binds me?

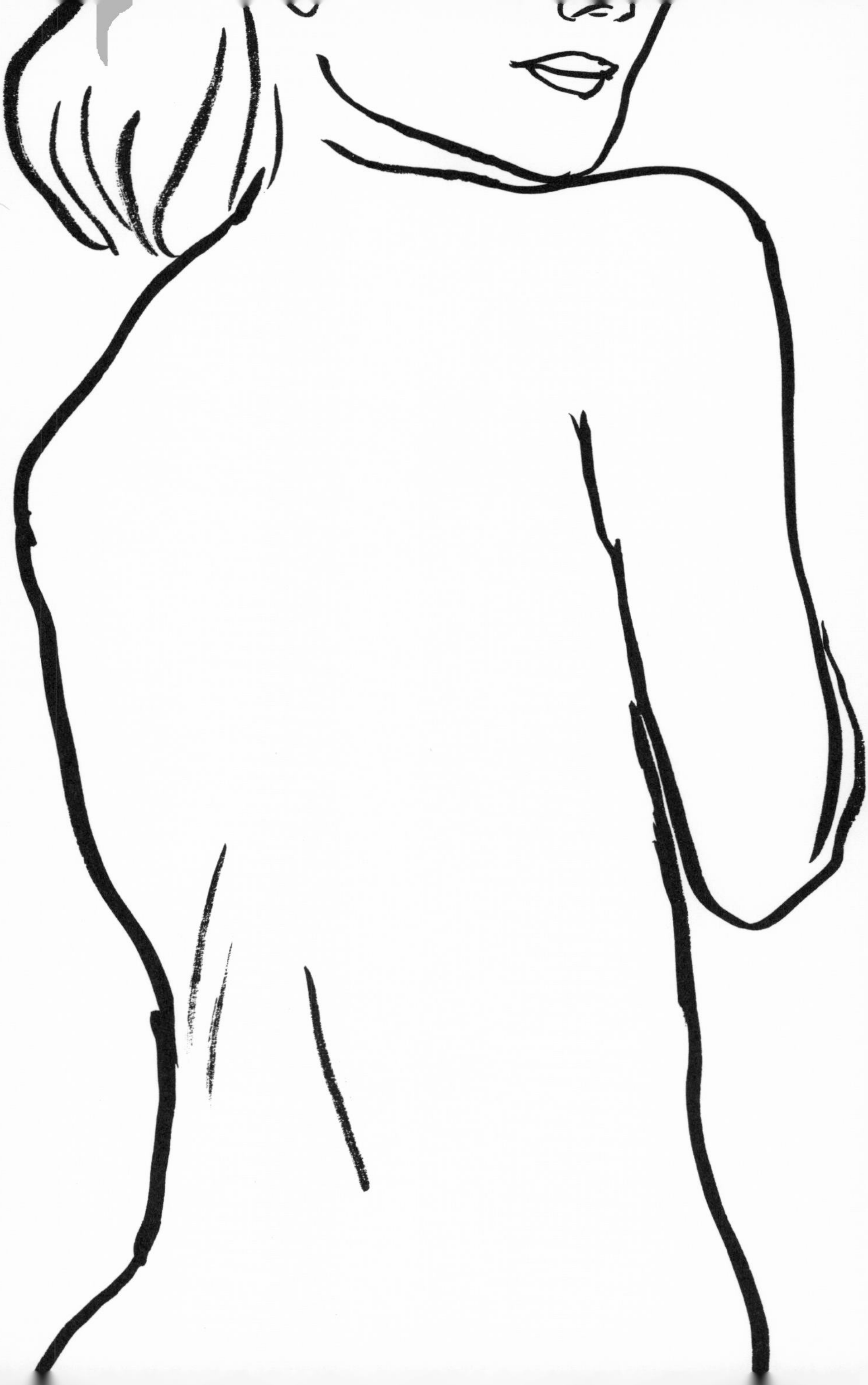

From what was
the chain formed
that bound the
Fenris Wolf?

It was made of
the noise of cats'
paws walking on
the ground,

of the beards
of women,

of the roots of
cliffs, of the grass
of bears, of the
breath of fish,
and the spittle
of birds.

I, too, am bound
in the same way
by a chain formed
of gloomy fancies,

of alarming
dreams,

of troubled
thoughts,

of fearful
presentiments,

of inexplicable
anxieties.

The chain is very flexible, soft as silk, yields to the most powerful strain.

and cannot be torn apart.

— SØREN KIERKEGAARD,
EITHER/OR: PART I

Jason's ex-girlfriend was Taylor.
She was from the South.

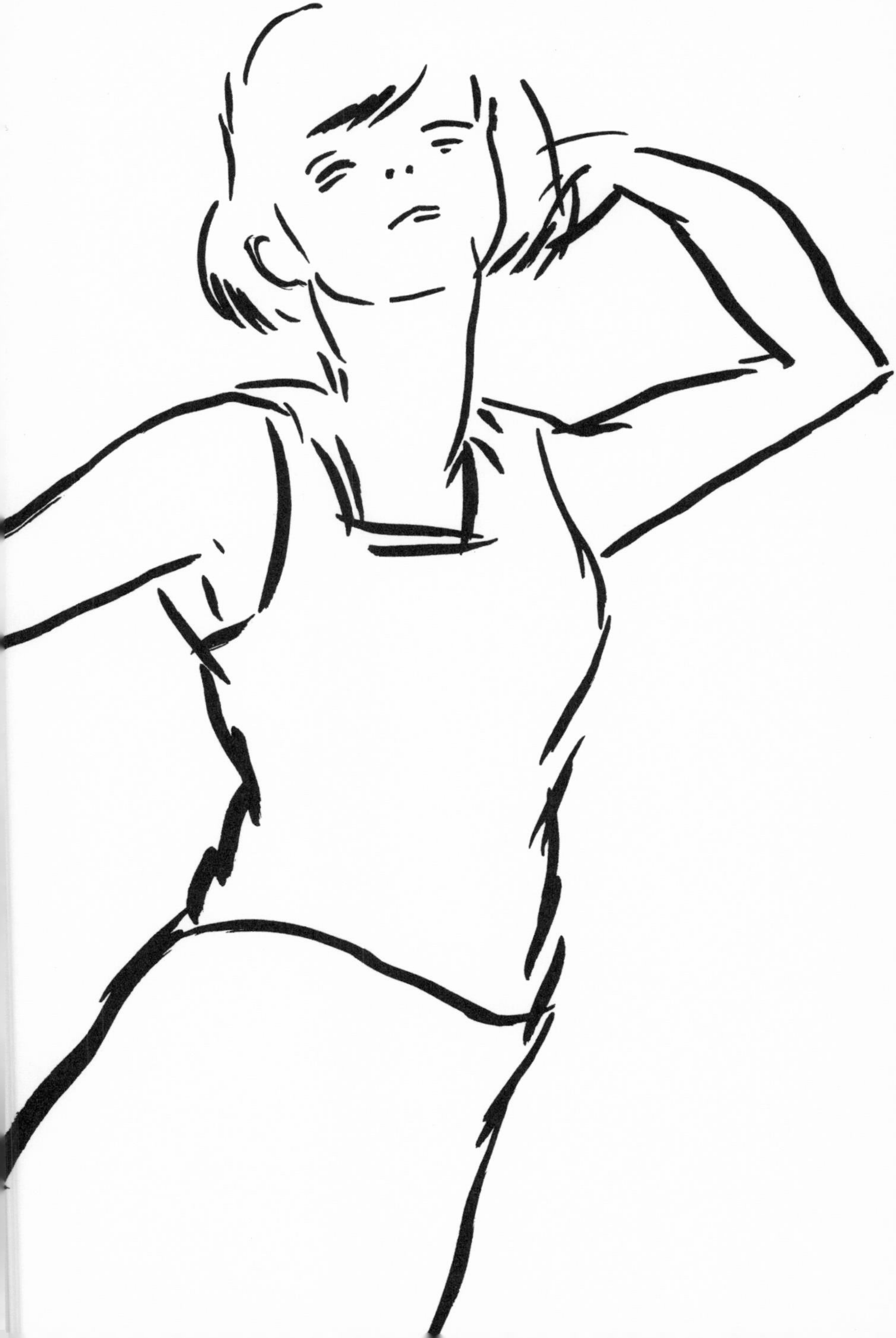

Leo's ex-girlfriend had a cult following.

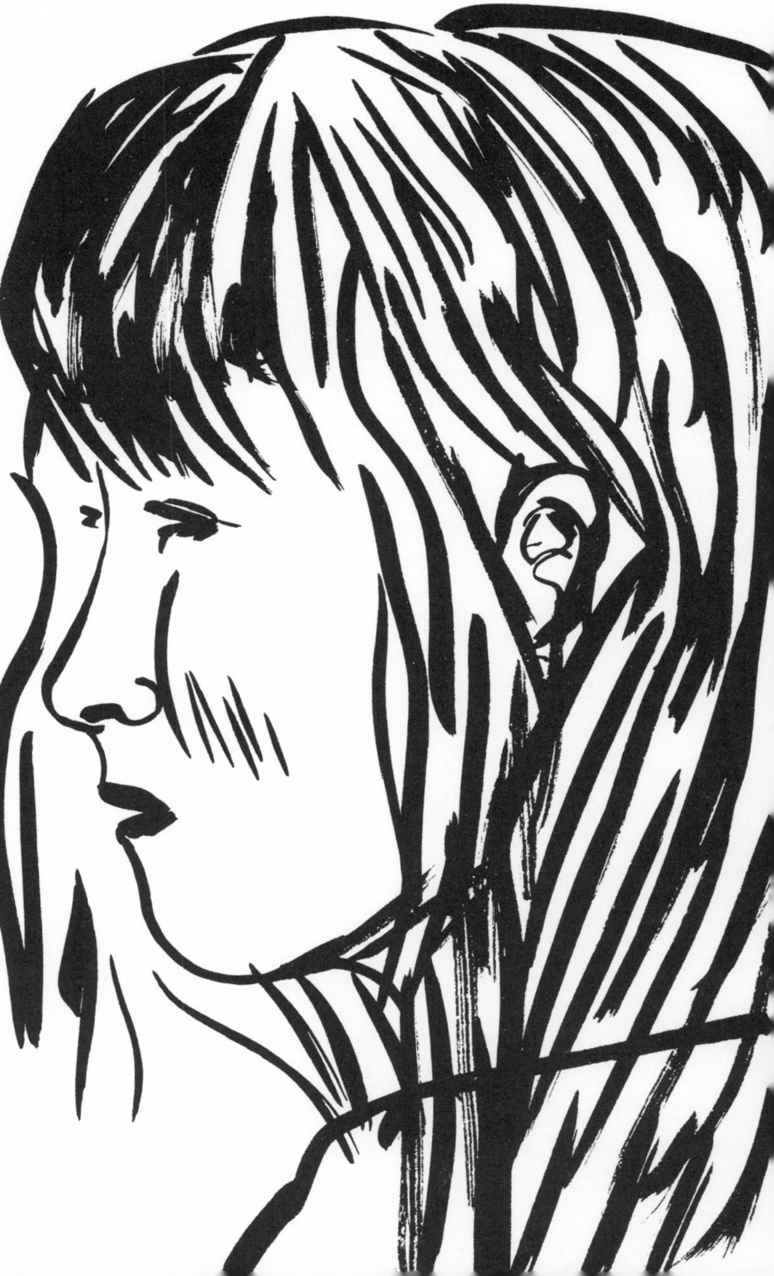

Monty's ex-girlfriend Weronika taught him how to speak Polish.

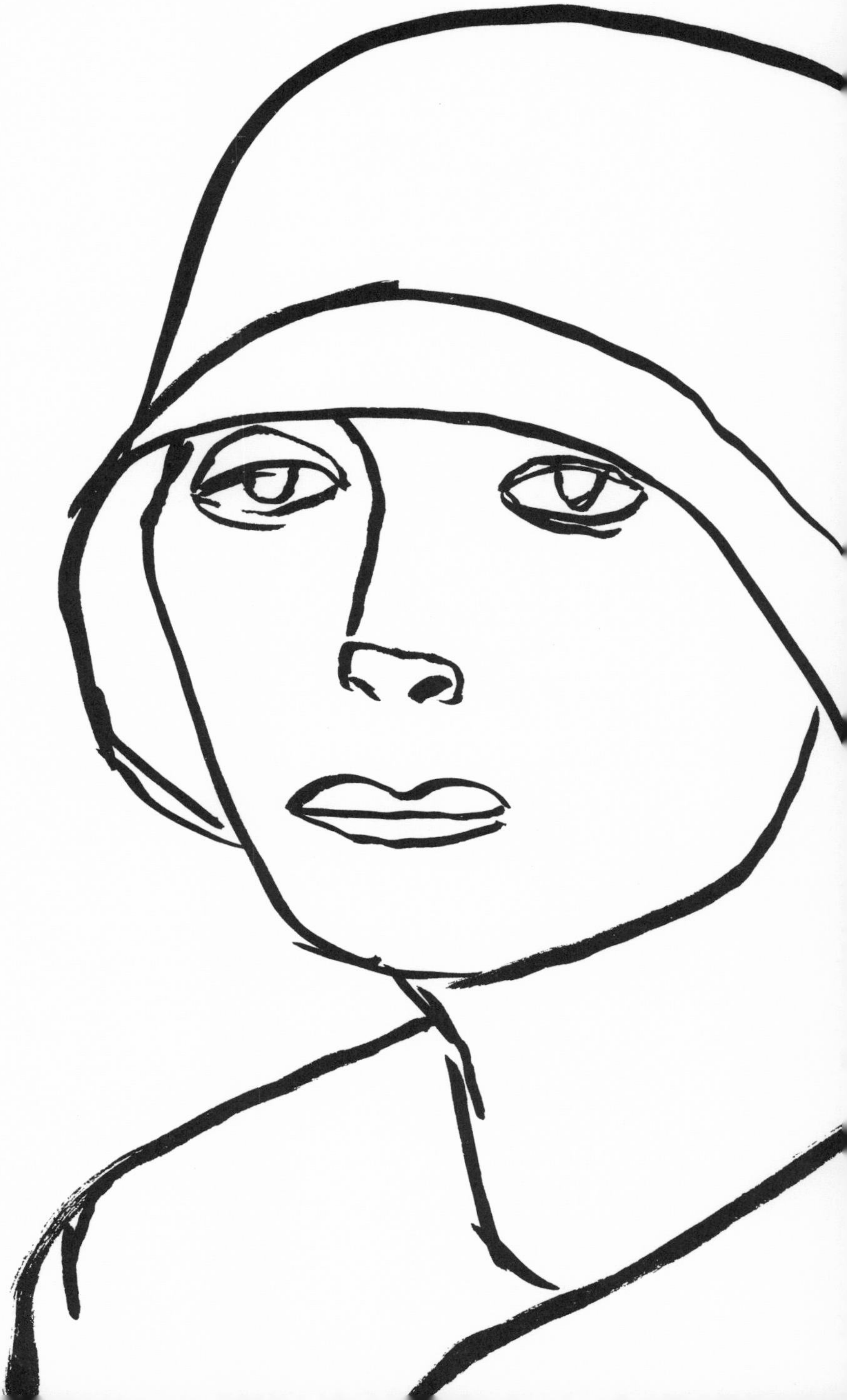

Nicholas's ex-girlfriend was a writer's writer.

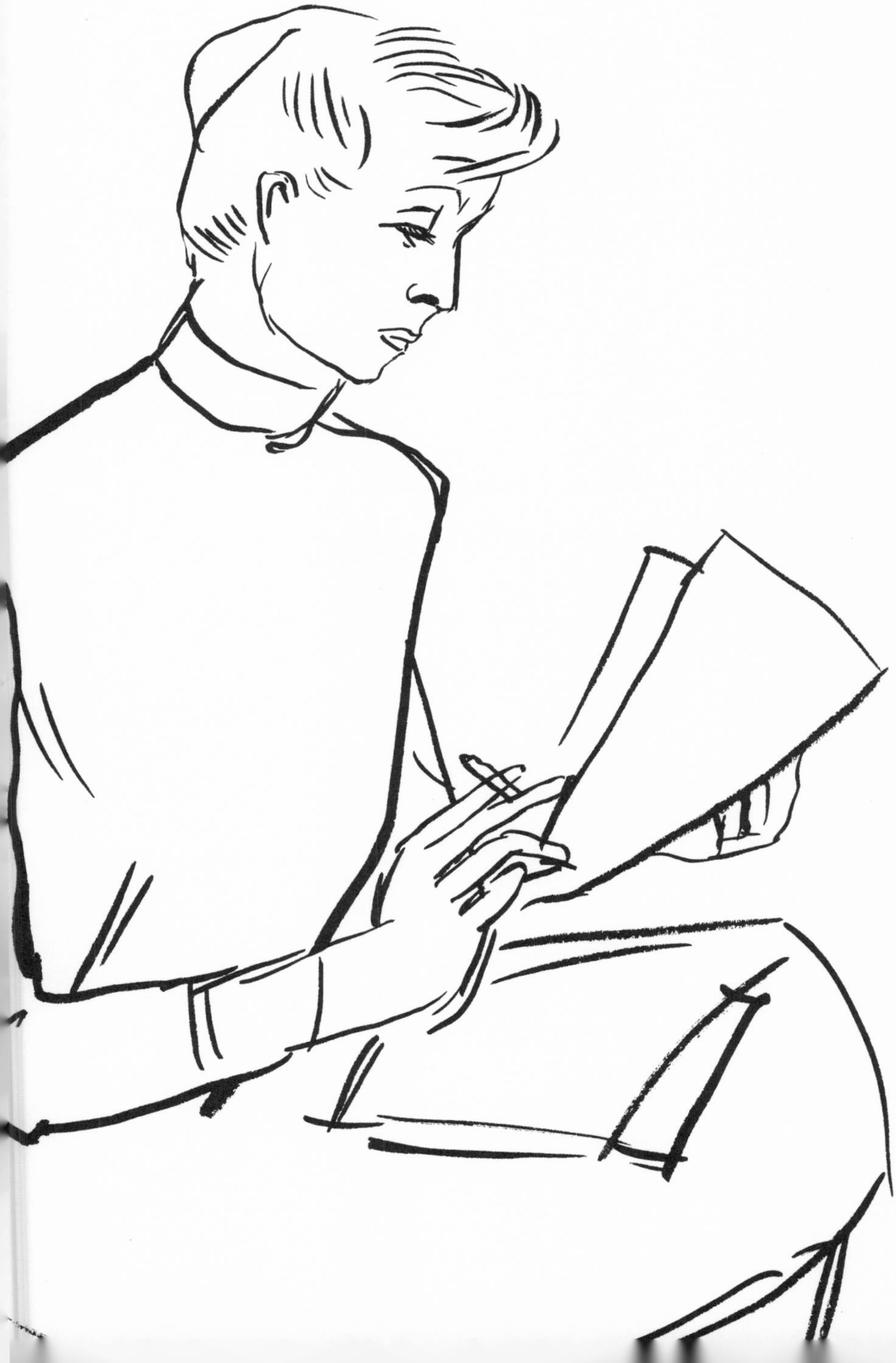

Colin's ex-girlfriend Heather was an independent feature film director who sometimes did videos. She once stated in an interview, "I couldn't make a blockbuster if I tried!"

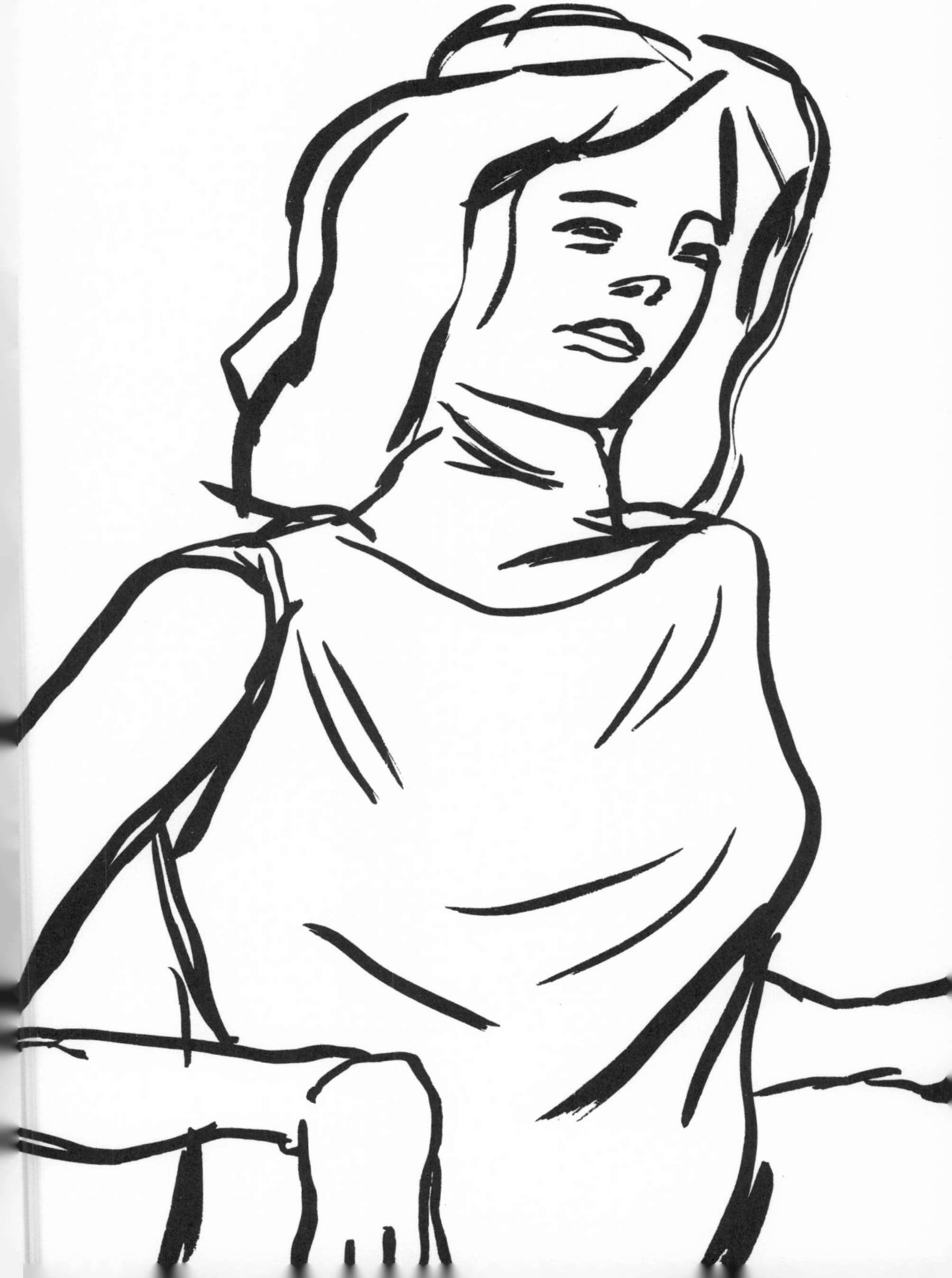

Heather's ex-boyfriend Joel wrote a novel based on their tempestuous and passionate relationship.

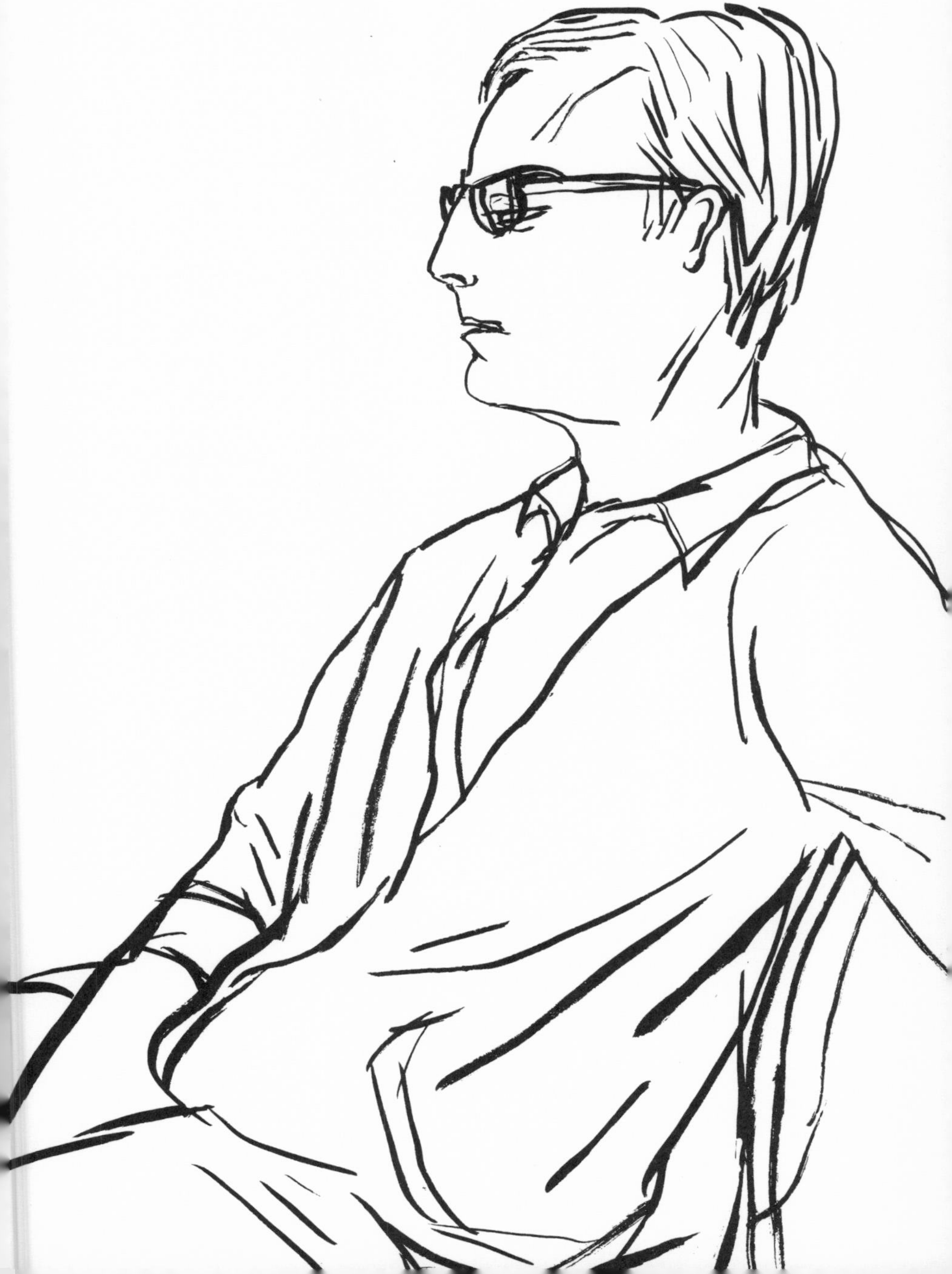

Joel's ex-girlfriend Marie was a concert pianist.
He described her hands as "quick and deft." Her
nails were painted with dark red Chanel varnish.

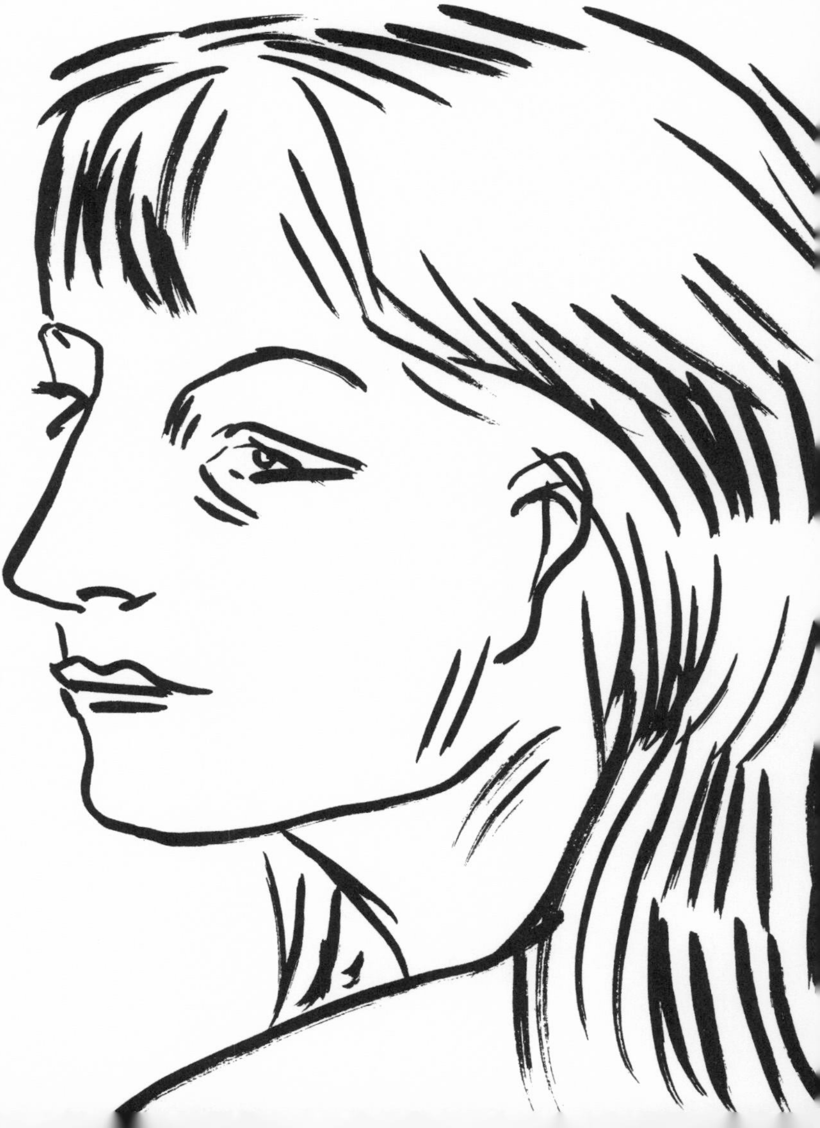

Marie's ex-boyfriend had chosen prog rock over a career in classical music.

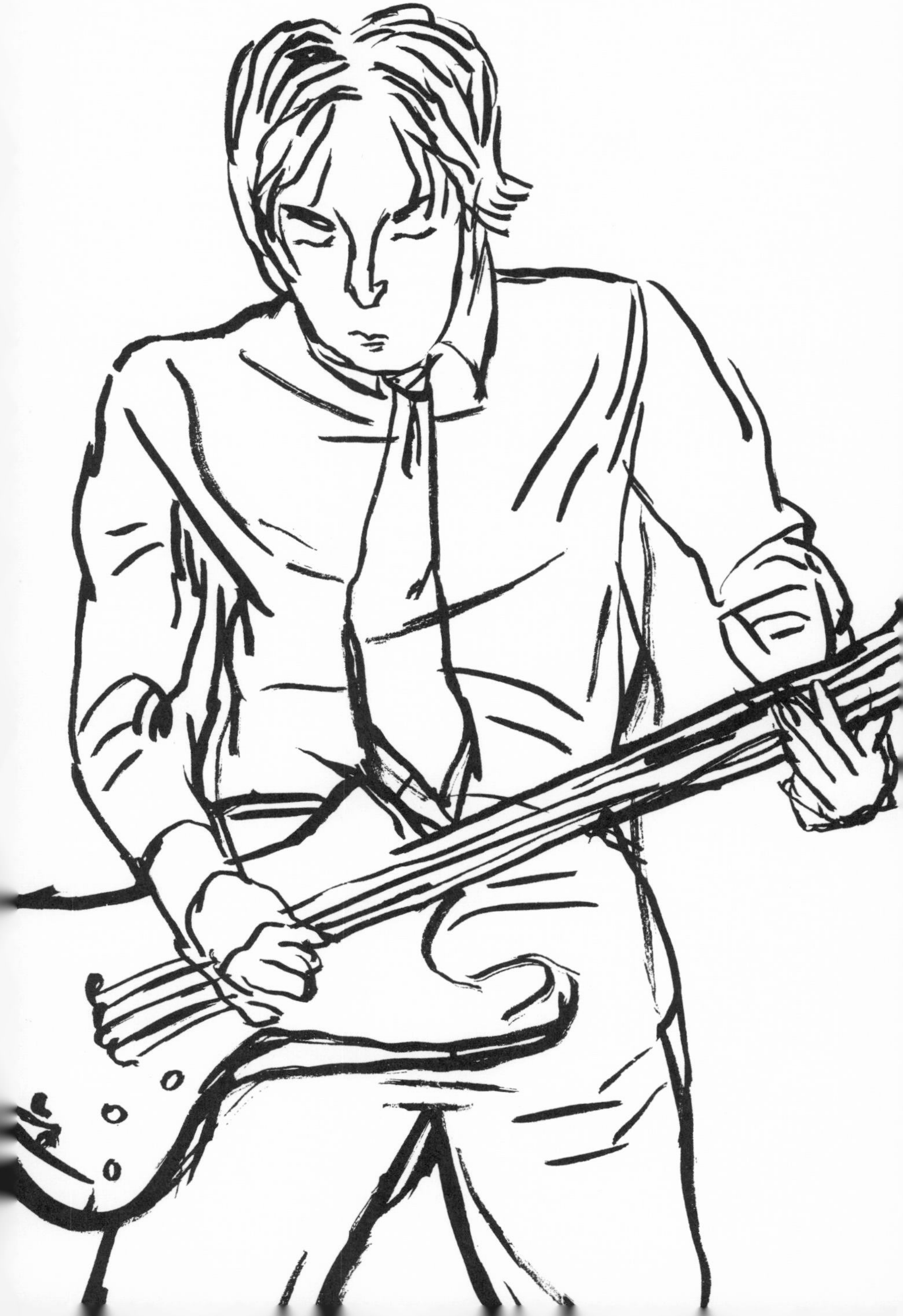

June's ex-boyfriend Wade kept his love
letters in a kitchen drawer. June was always
tempted, but never opened the drawer.
She would stare at it while she cooked.

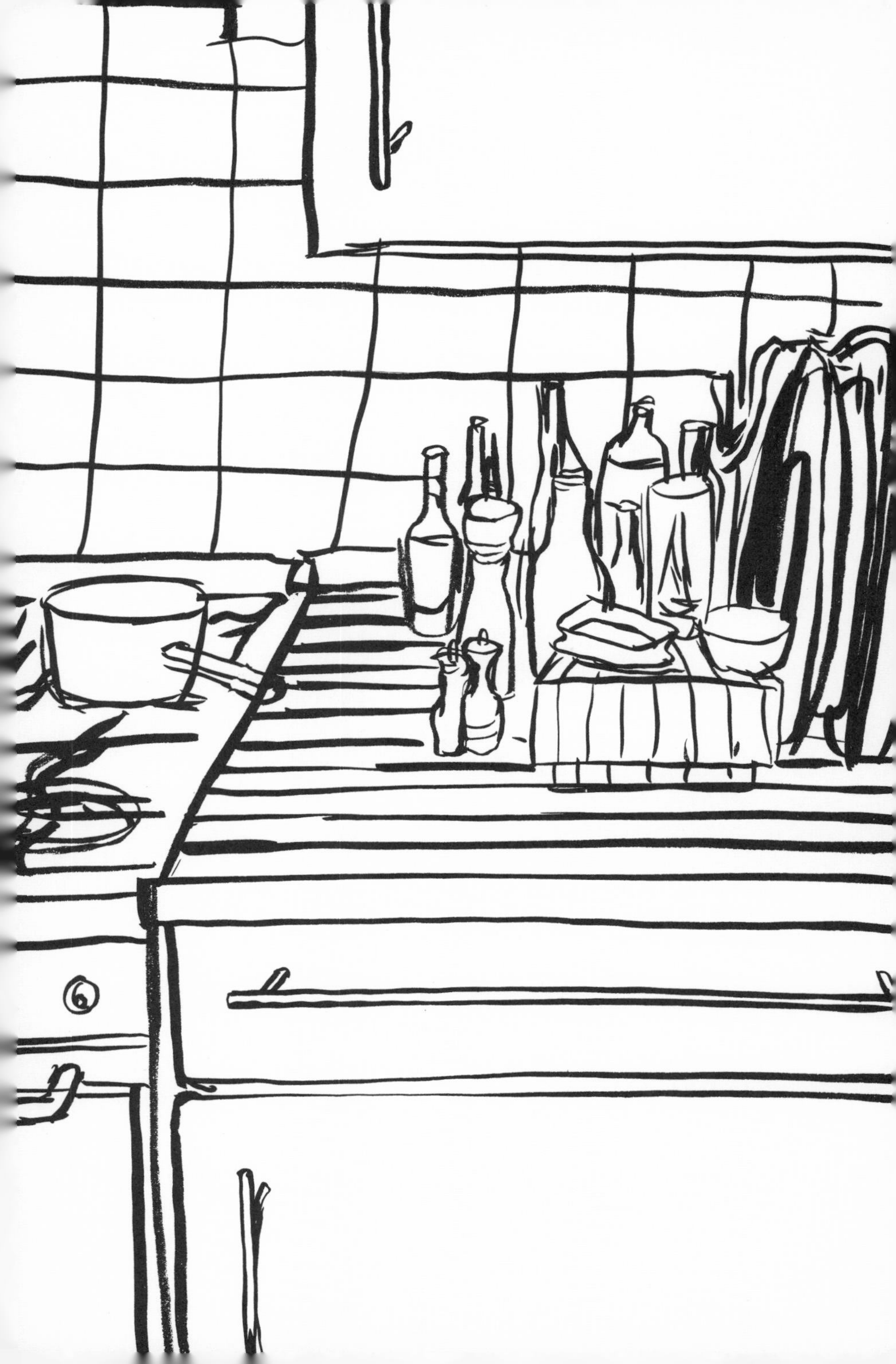

Wade's ex-girlfriend Siobhan was a poet who moved to a small northern town near Lake Superior with her son.

Alasdair's ex-girlfriend was his first cousin Annabel.
Their family was very casual about it all. They were a
close-knit clan of eccentric and photogenic aristocrats
who often modeled for luxury ad campaigns.

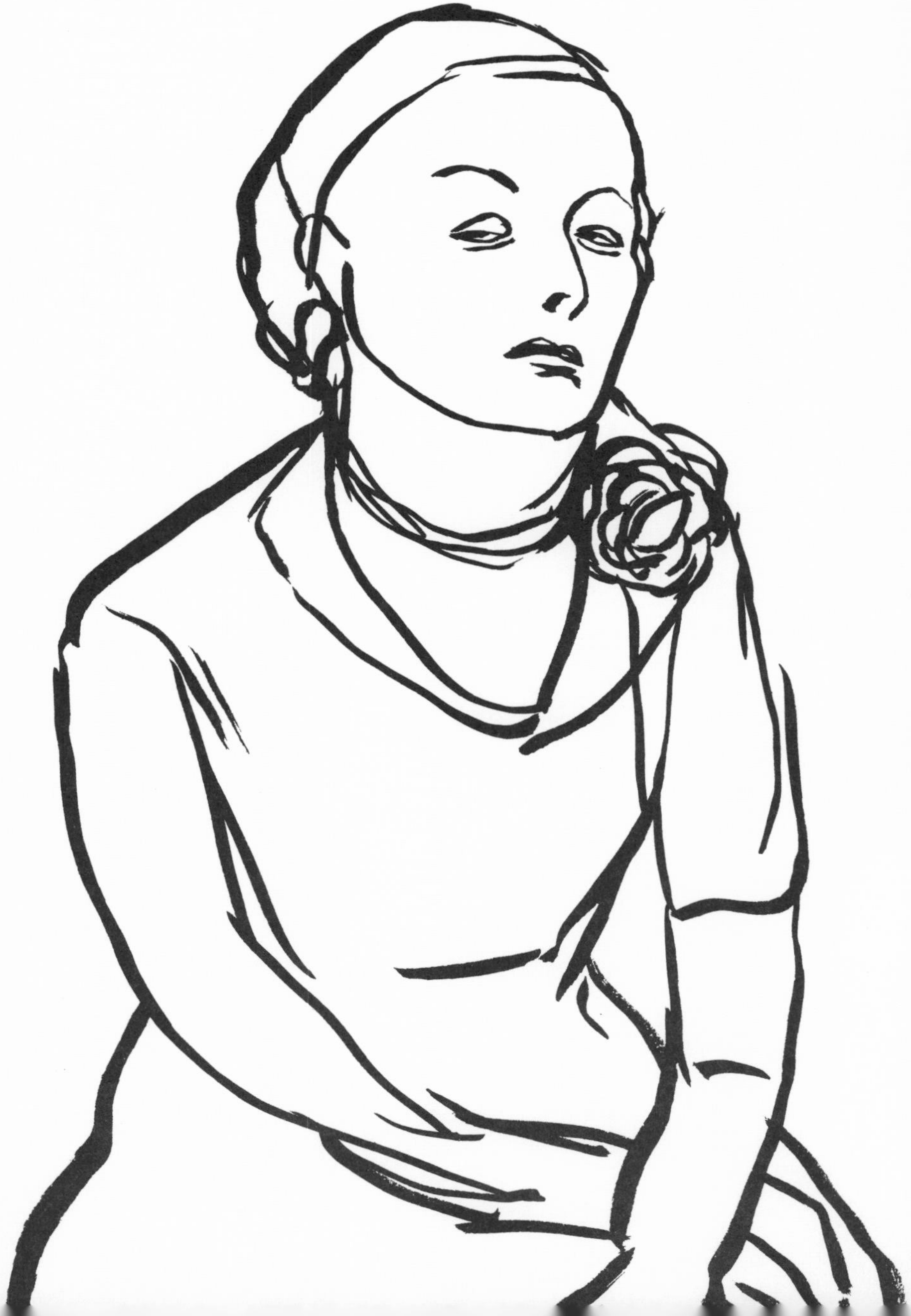

Ben's ex-girlfriend Lara was a physiotherapist for the Canadian men's and women's Olympic swim teams. She wore small white shorts year-round.

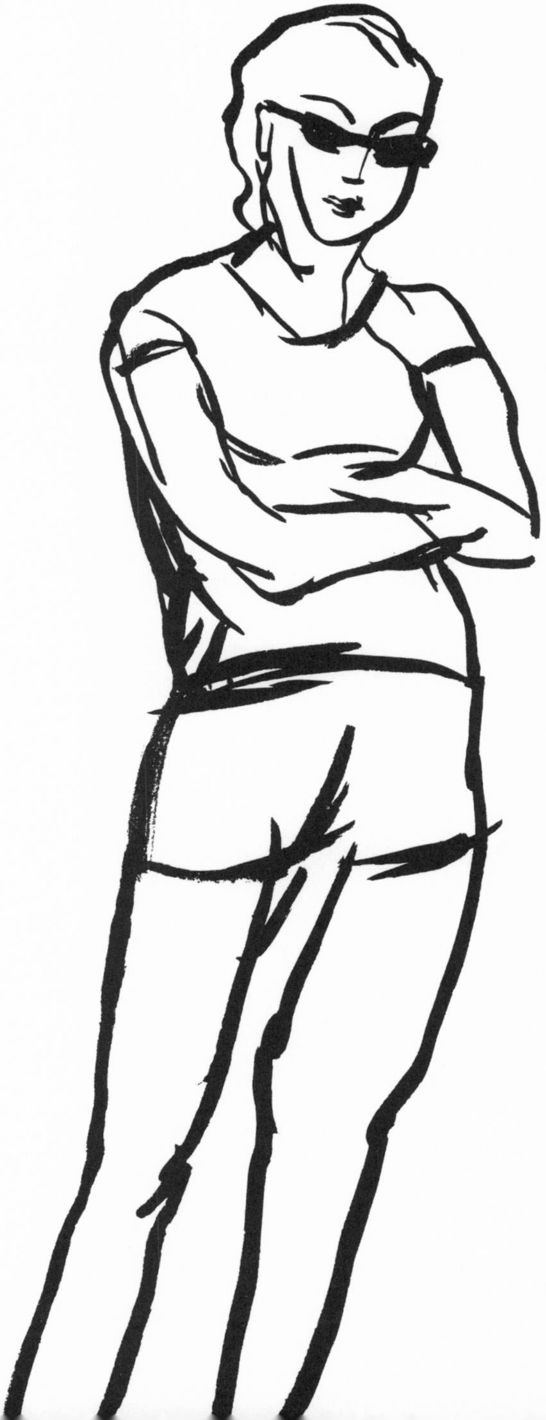

Greg's ex-girlfriend was Lucy. She was a British actress living in LA. She had perfect features, but was always told she was too pretty for roles.

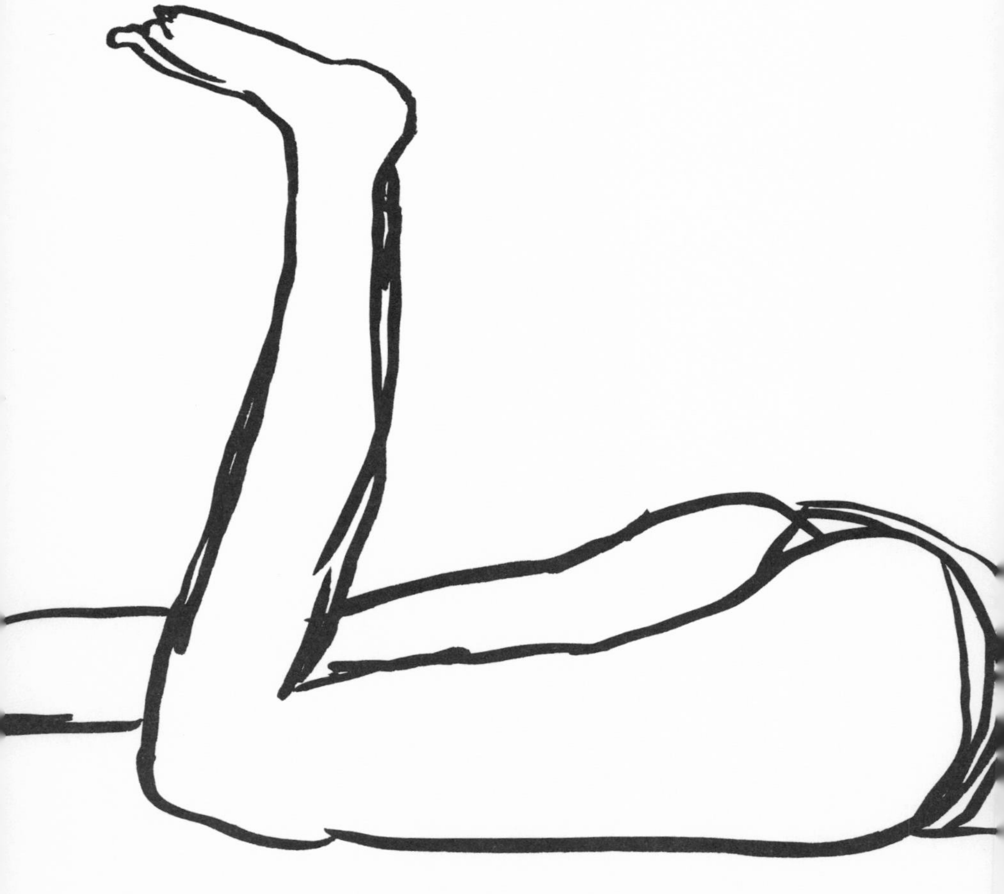

Lucy's ex-boyfriend only dated actresses.
It didn't matter to him if they got roles, but
he was happy for them if they did.

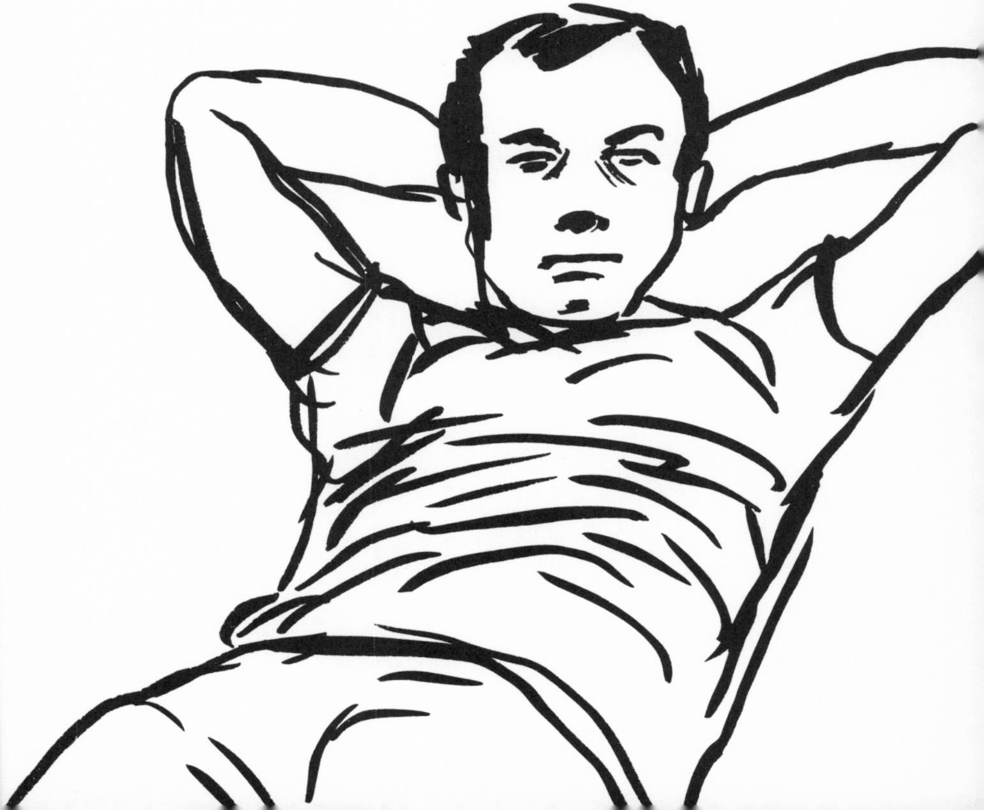

Hugo's ex-girlfriend Katya was 70 percent deaf.
She had a gentle way with children and animals.

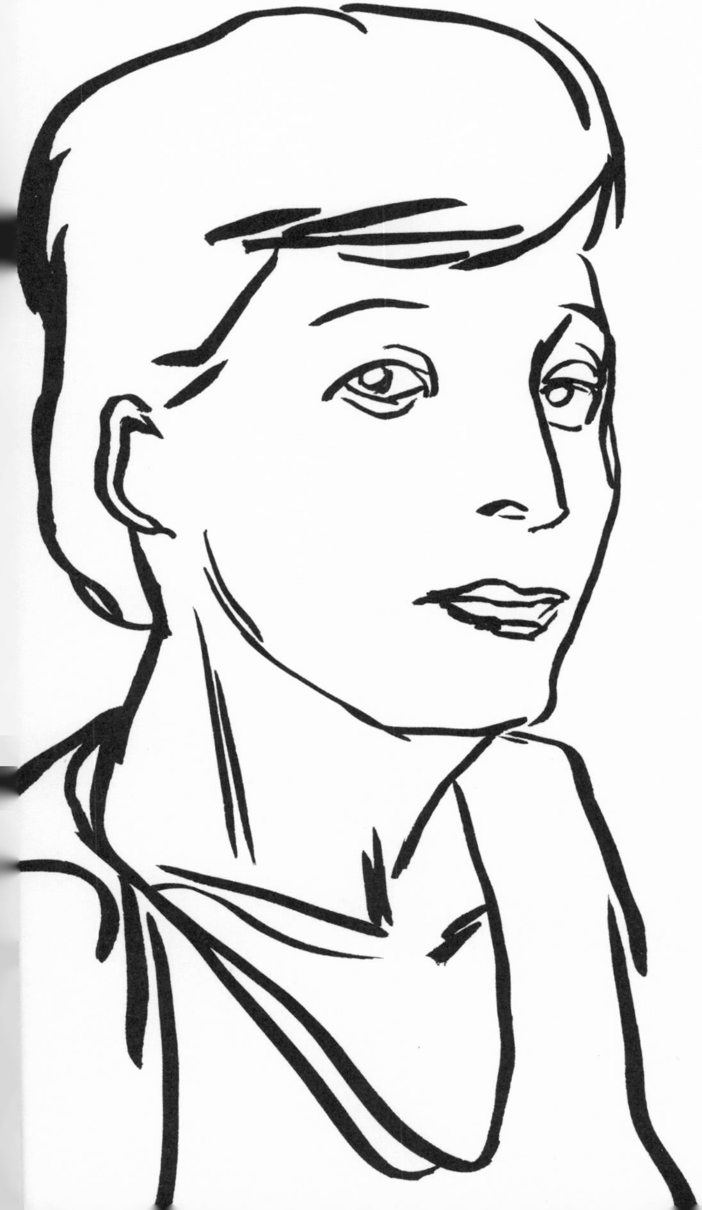

Katya's ex-boyfriend never stopped sending
her postcards.

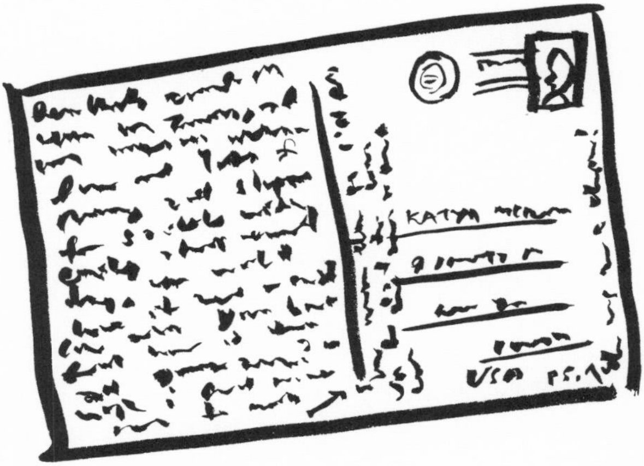
KATYA
USA

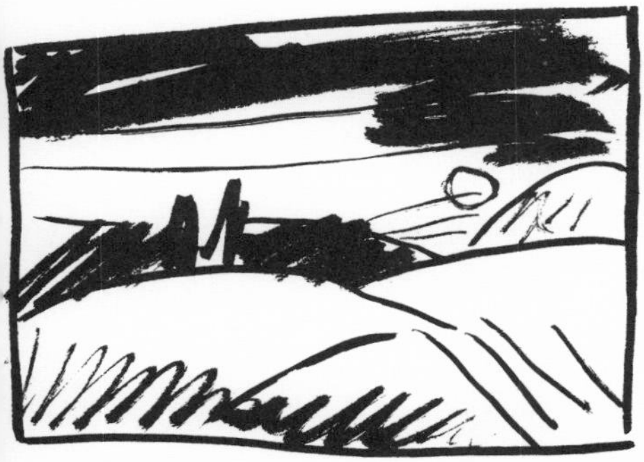

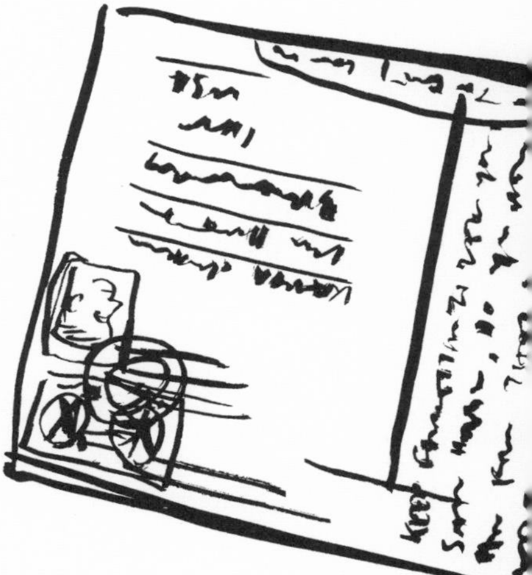

Glen's ex-girlfriend Vanessa was an activist. She was imprisoned for twenty days in a Paris jail for leading a demonstration, and was photographed in her cell by a famous photojournalist. The image of Vanessa looking defiant and beautiful in her dirty T-shirt was published worldwide and won numerous awards.

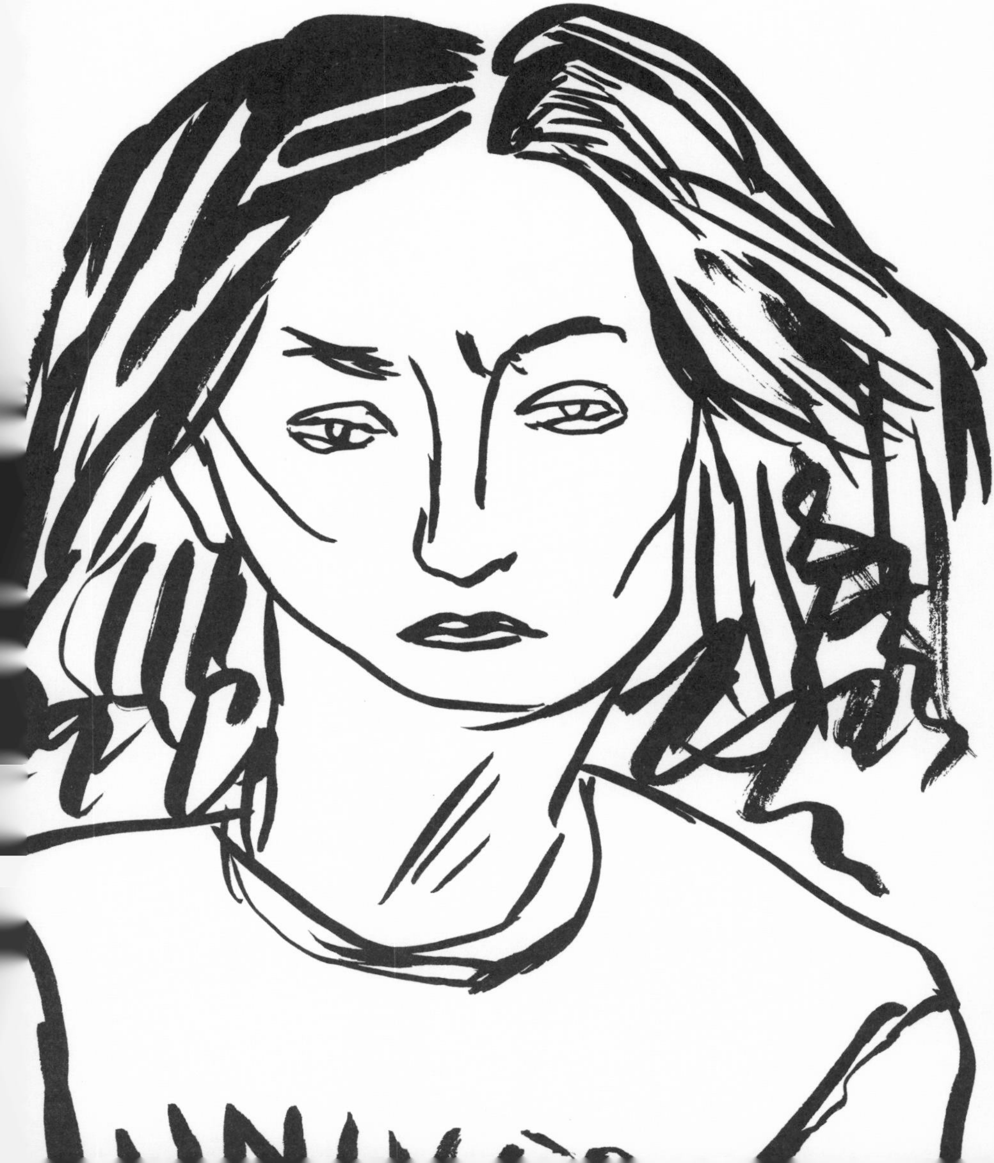

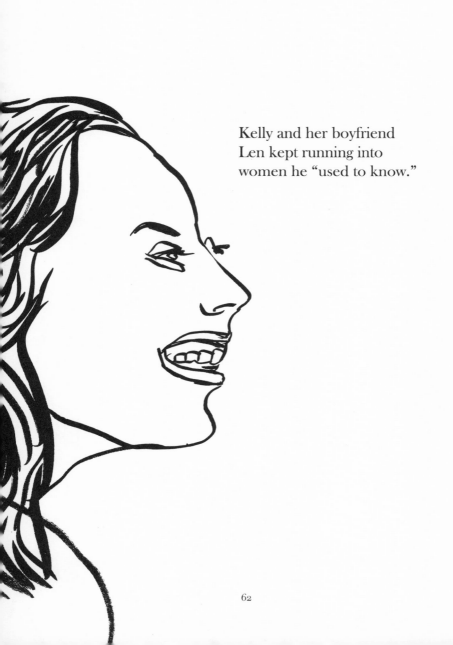

Kelly and her boyfriend
Len kept running into
women he "used to know."

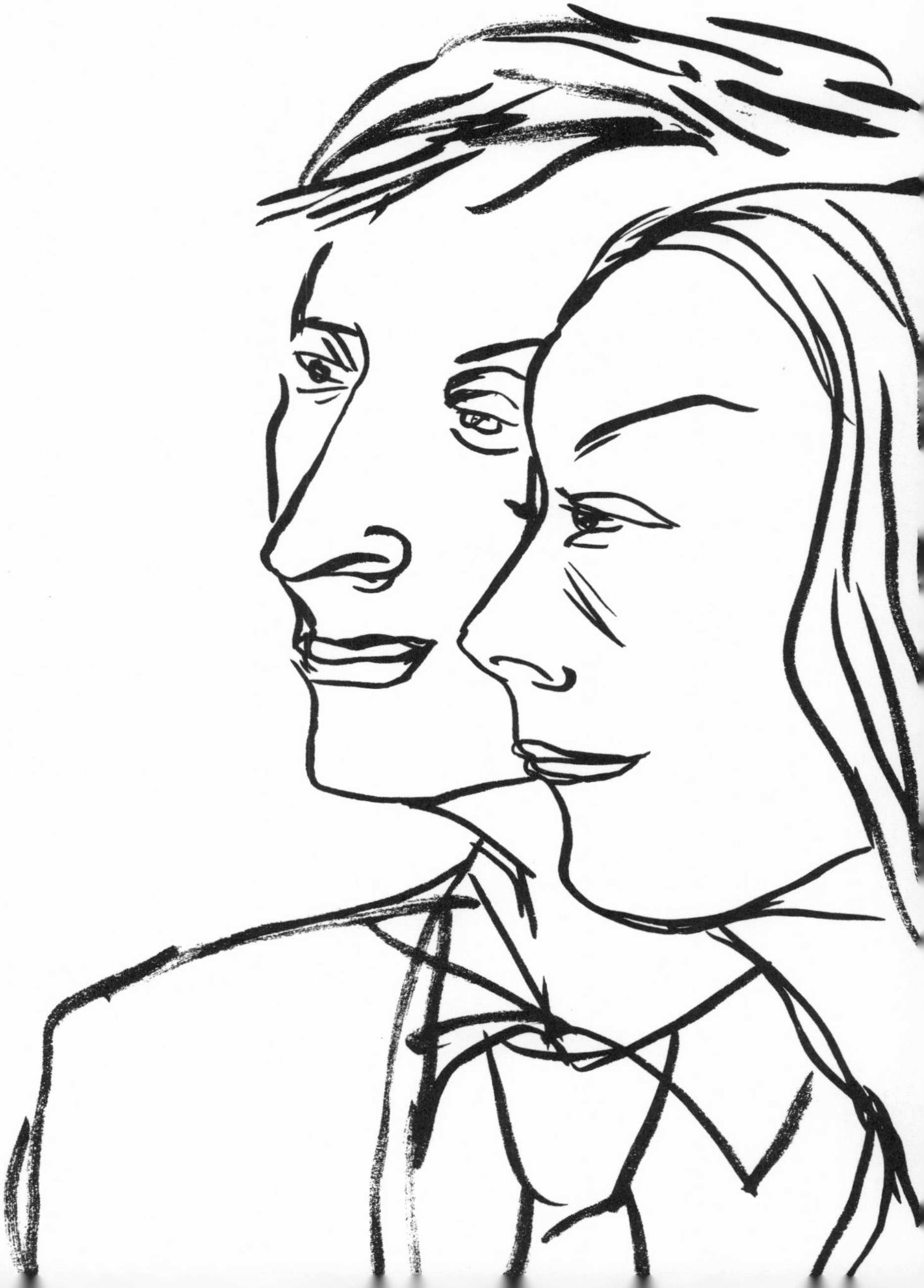

One of the women Len used to know was an opinionated academic. She wore braces and they looked fantastic.

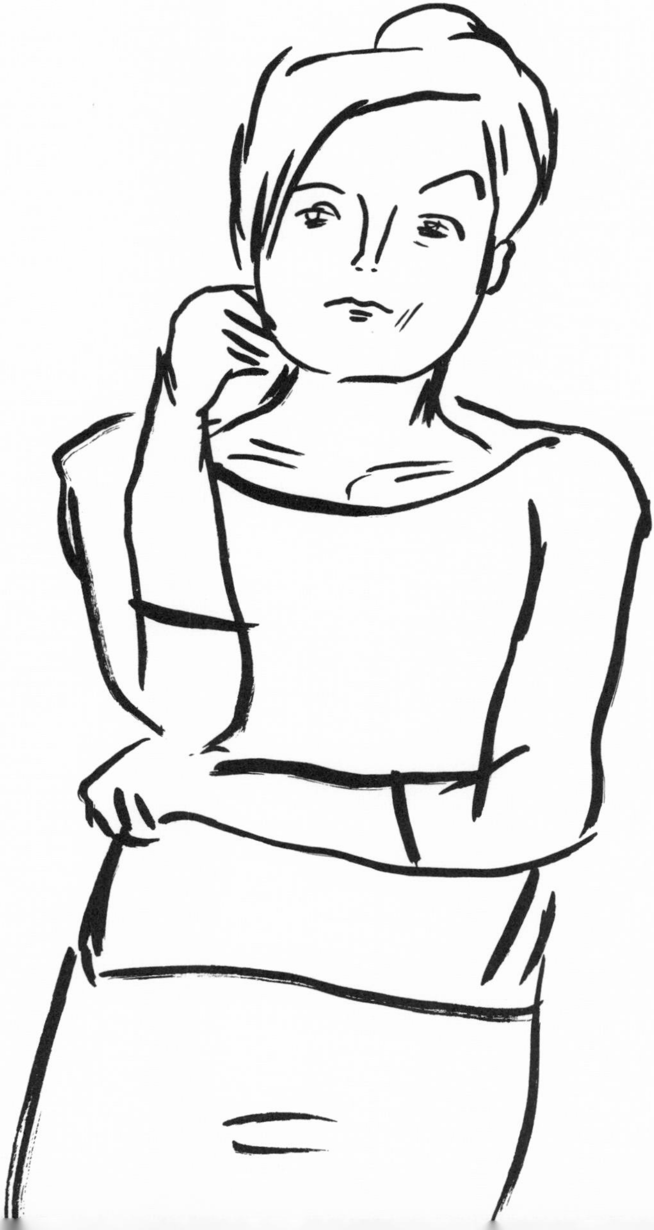

Another posed for life drawing classes.

Jonathan's ex-girlfriend was Constance. She was a nurse. She hated her uniform, but Jonathan loved it.

Colleen was Walter's ex-girlfriend from med school. She loved to dance with men at weddings.

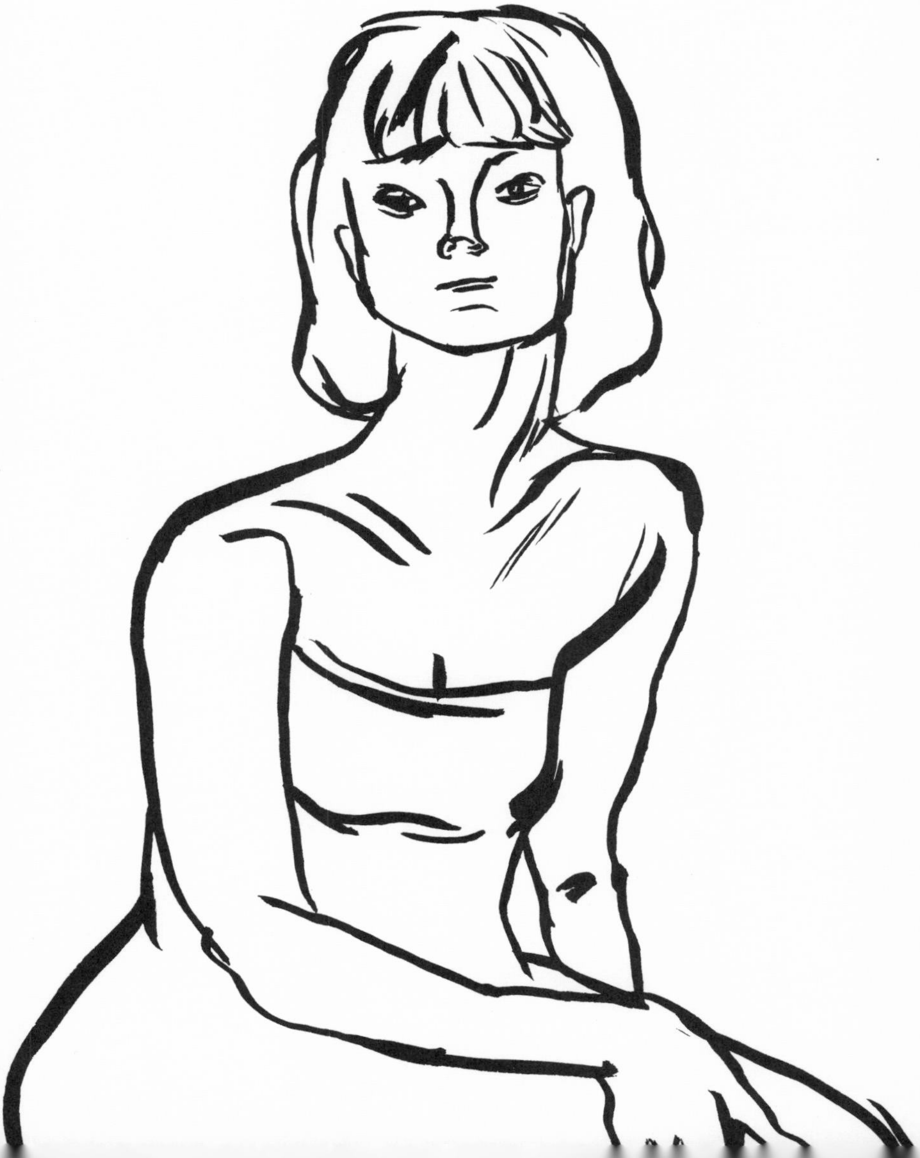

Martin had never mentioned his hauntingly beautiful ex-girlfriend Carwai to Heidi.

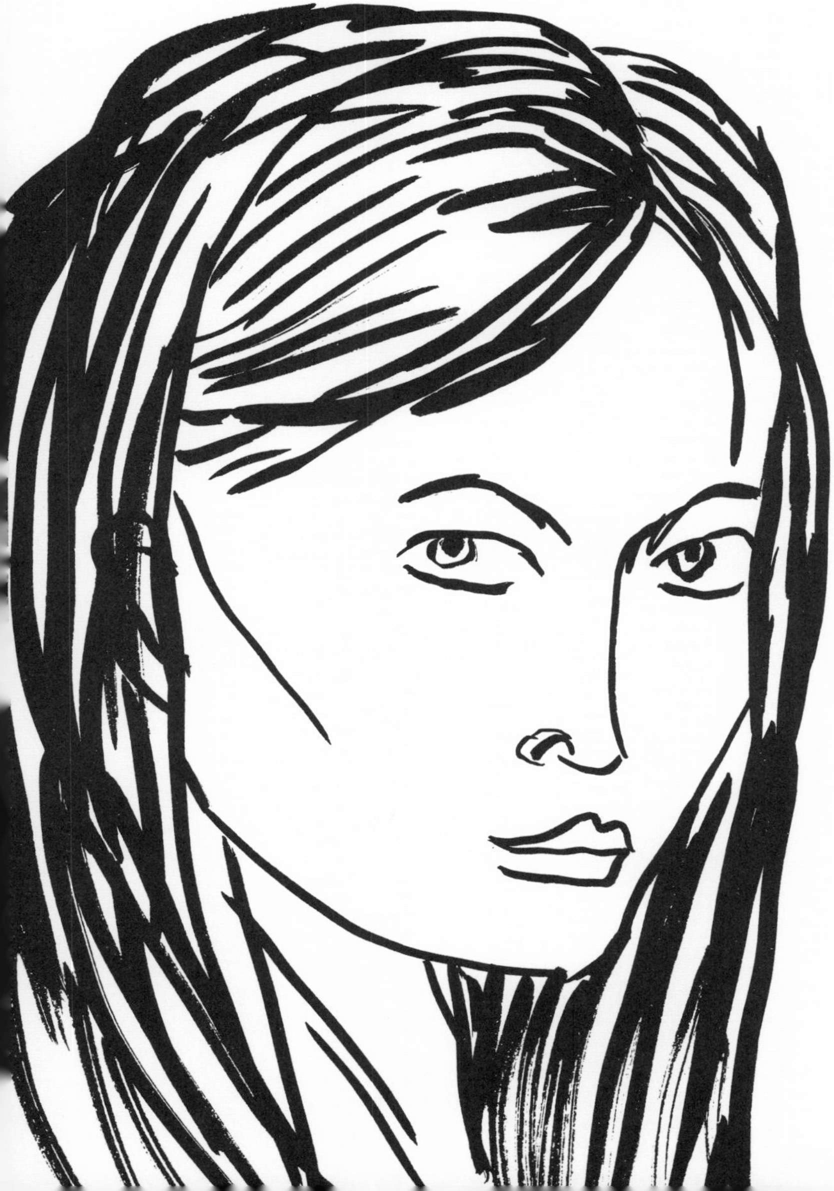

When Carwai called one night, Martin took the telephone to another room and shut the door.

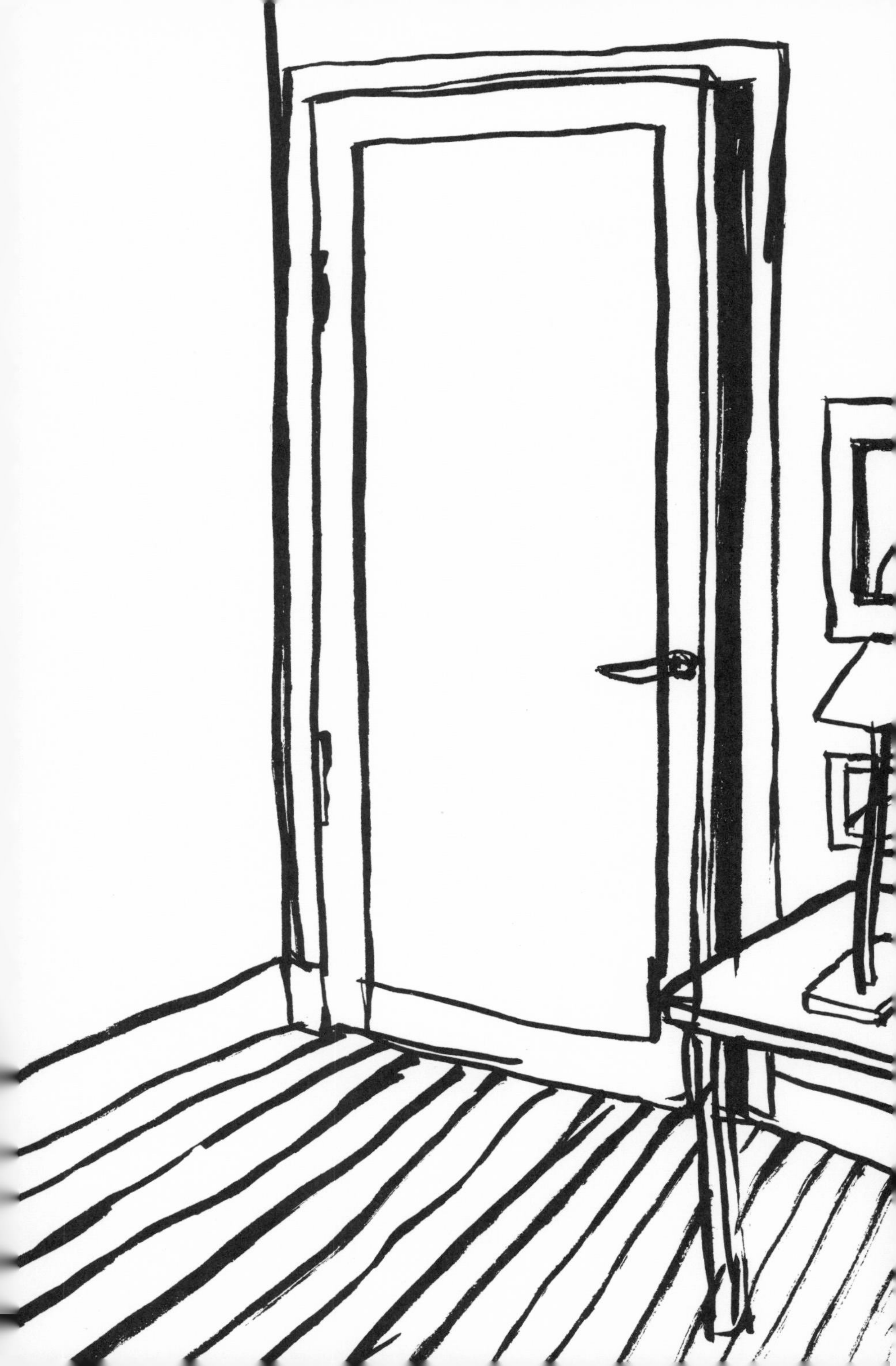

Josephine had a recurring dream. In it, Robert's ex-girlfriend Alicia kept trying to give Josephine articles of used clothing.

Jennifer's boyfriend Richard had a vast and expensive wardrobe. Most of his shirts had been chosen for him by his ex-girlfriend Cassandra.

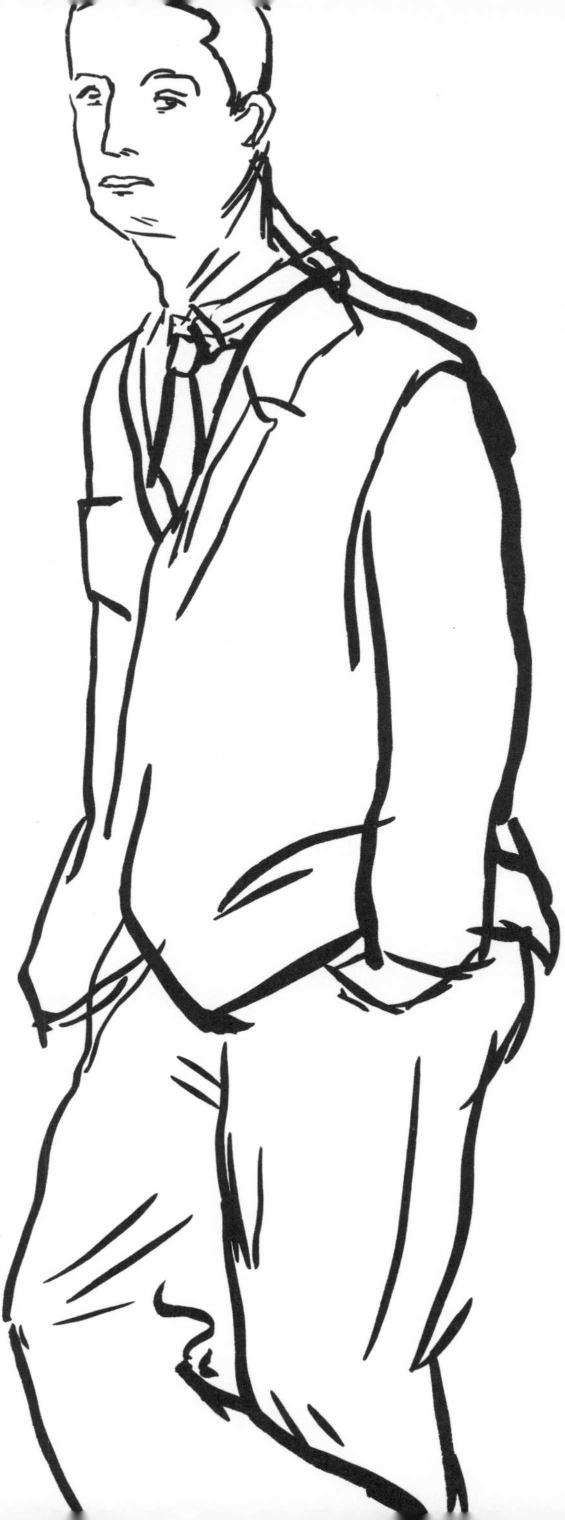

Cassandra was the daughter of two prominent psychoanalysts. She was very conscientious. She did yoga, jogged, took ballet classes, did Pilates, swam lengths, and had regular acupuncture. She dreaded meeting any woman thinner than her. She studied herself in every reflective surface she passed.

Sebastian's ex-girlfriend Makeda often mentioned she was descended from Ethiopian royalty.

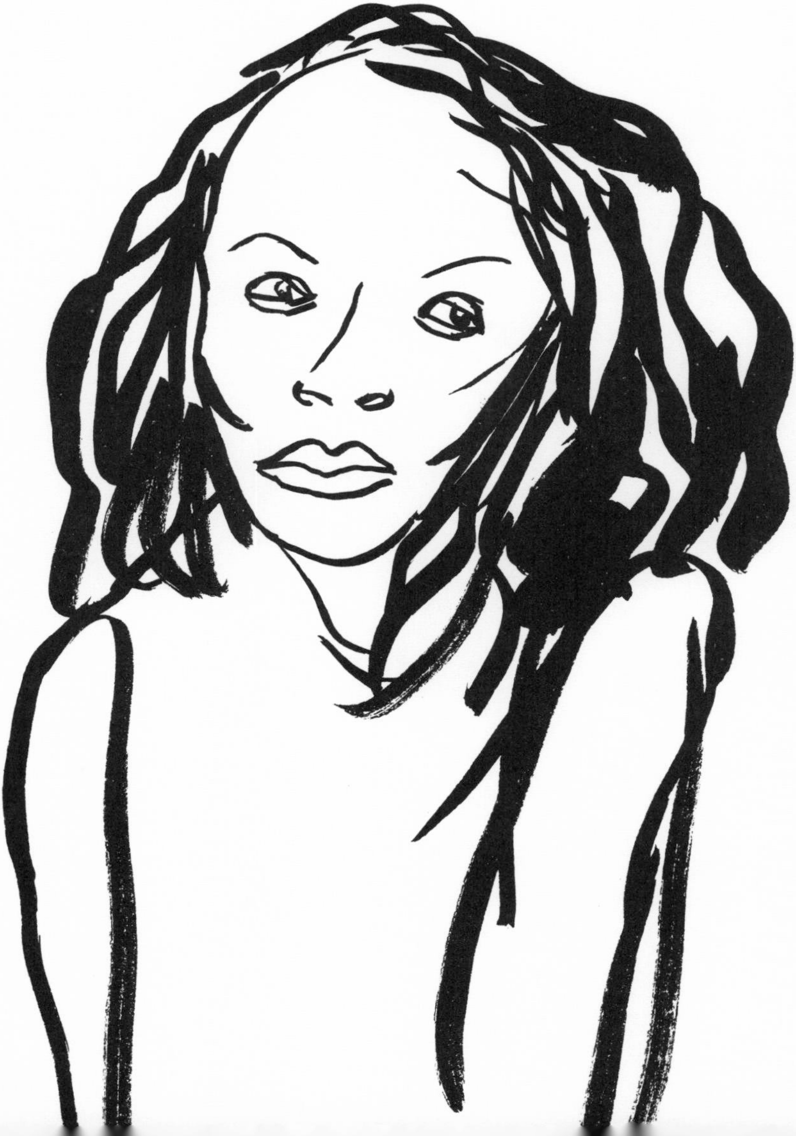

Makeda's ex-boyfriend Bruce collected African art. She always felt a little funny lying in his bed surrounded by his tribal jewelry and teak sculptures.

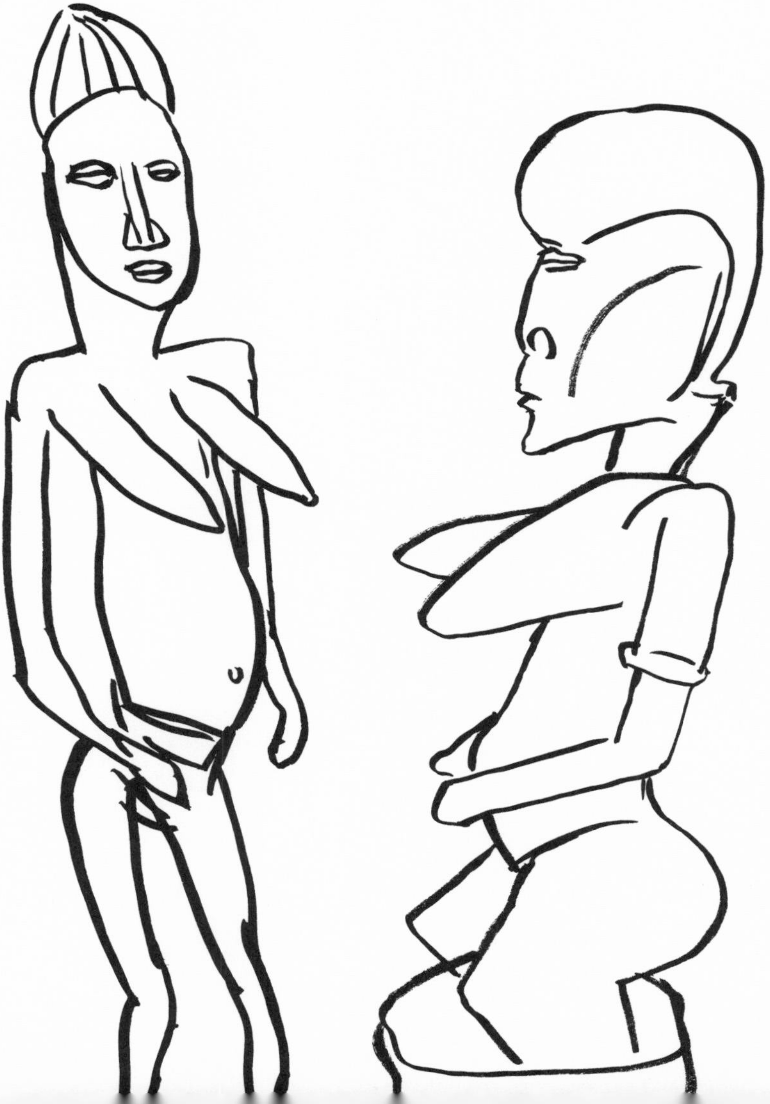

Noah's ex-girlfriend Clara was exceptionally beautiful but refused to acknowledge it. She wore baggy pants and many layers of turtlenecks and sweaters, but this modesty made her seem even more beautiful.

Sheldon's ex-girlfriend was Dianna.
She was uninhibited.

To his friends, family, and girlfriend, Anton's ex-girlfriend was known only as "The Ballerina."

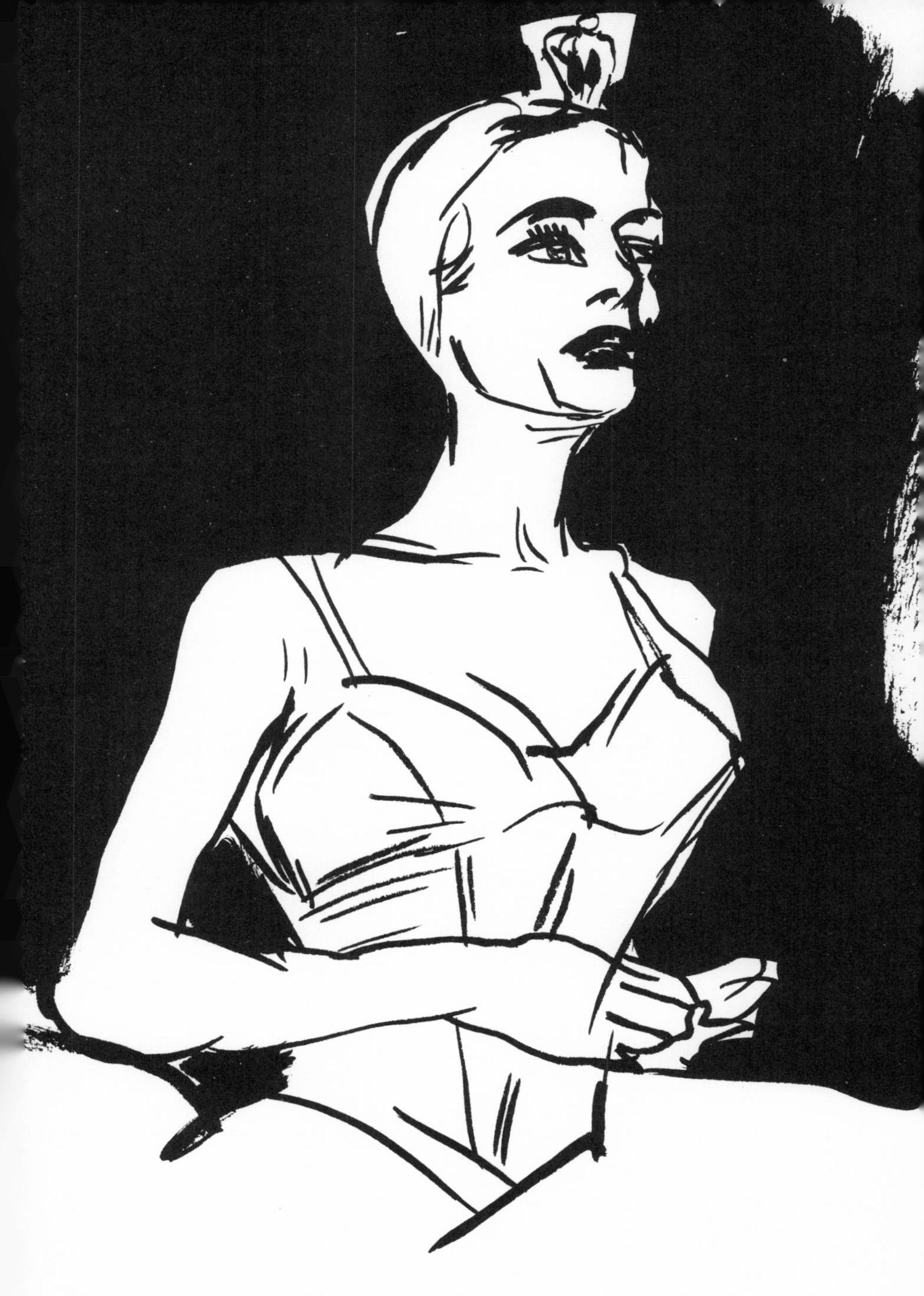

Jacob's parents adored his ex-girlfriend Cynthia.

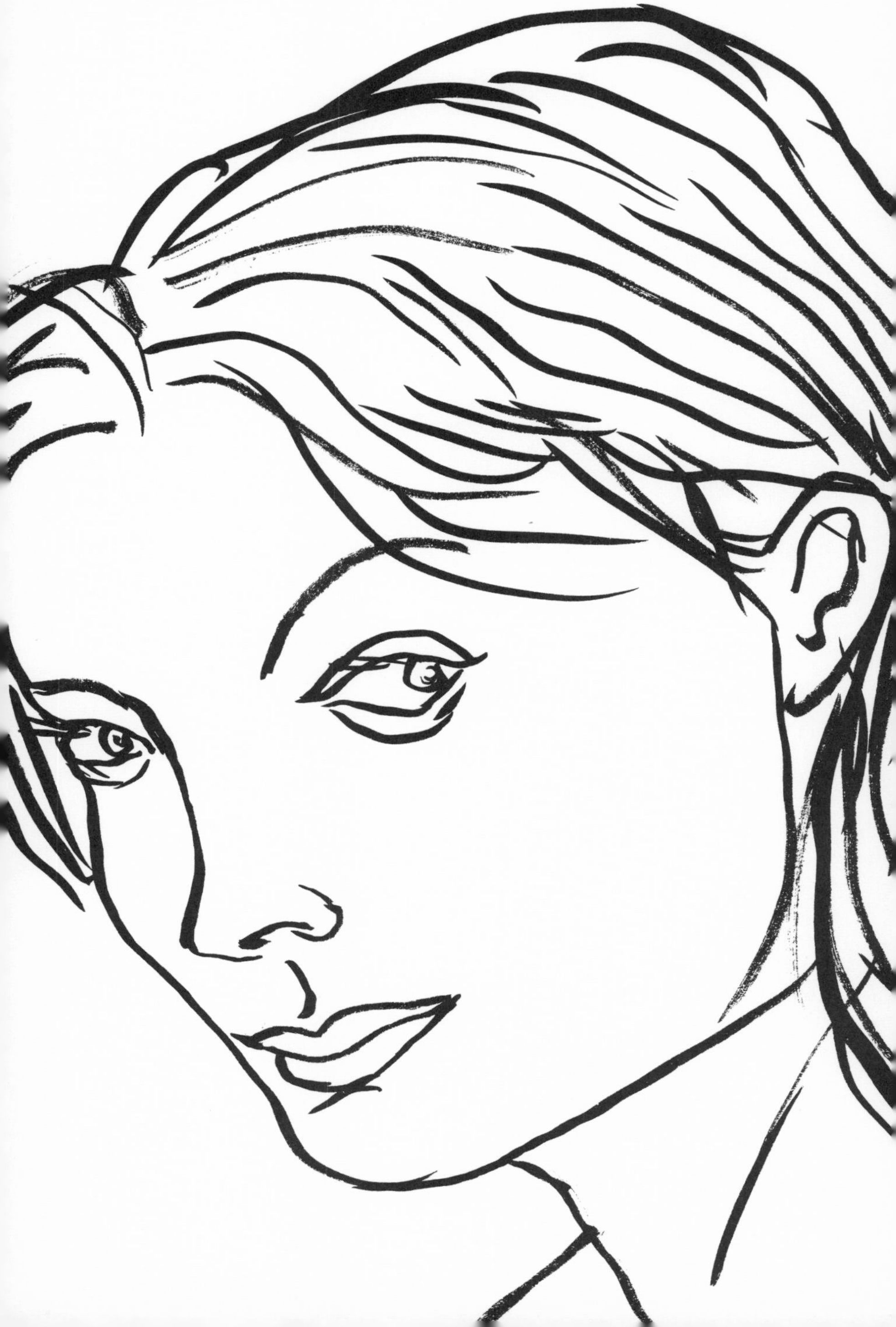

Steve's ex-girlfriend Nicola got him interested in S&M.

Graham kept a number of girlfriends on the go. He made them all the same mixed CD—a compilation of romantic and meaningful songs.

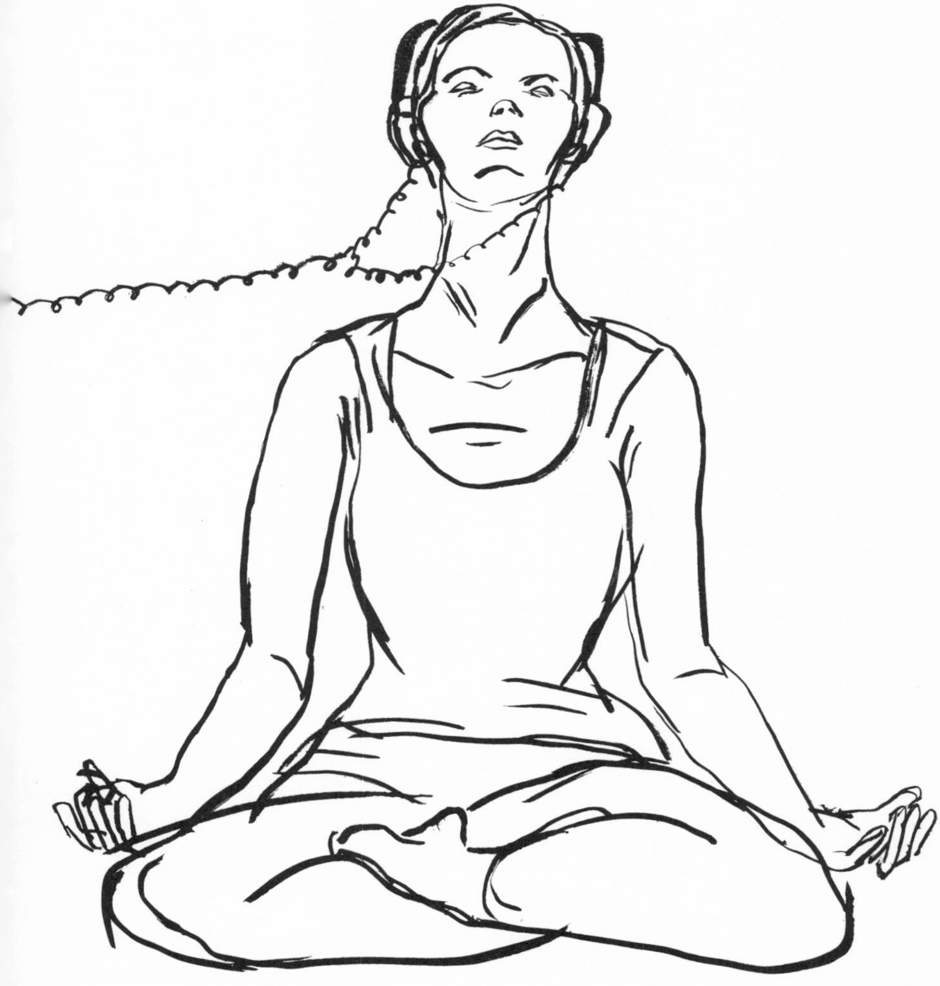

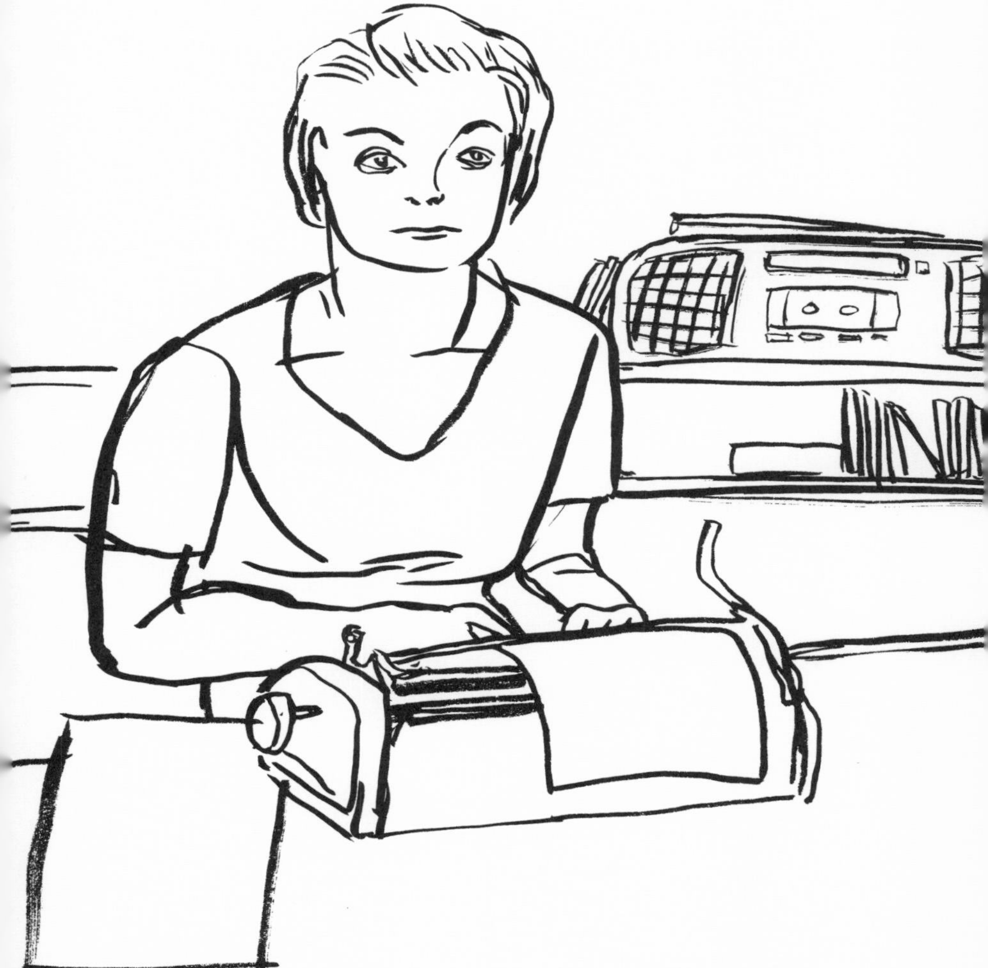

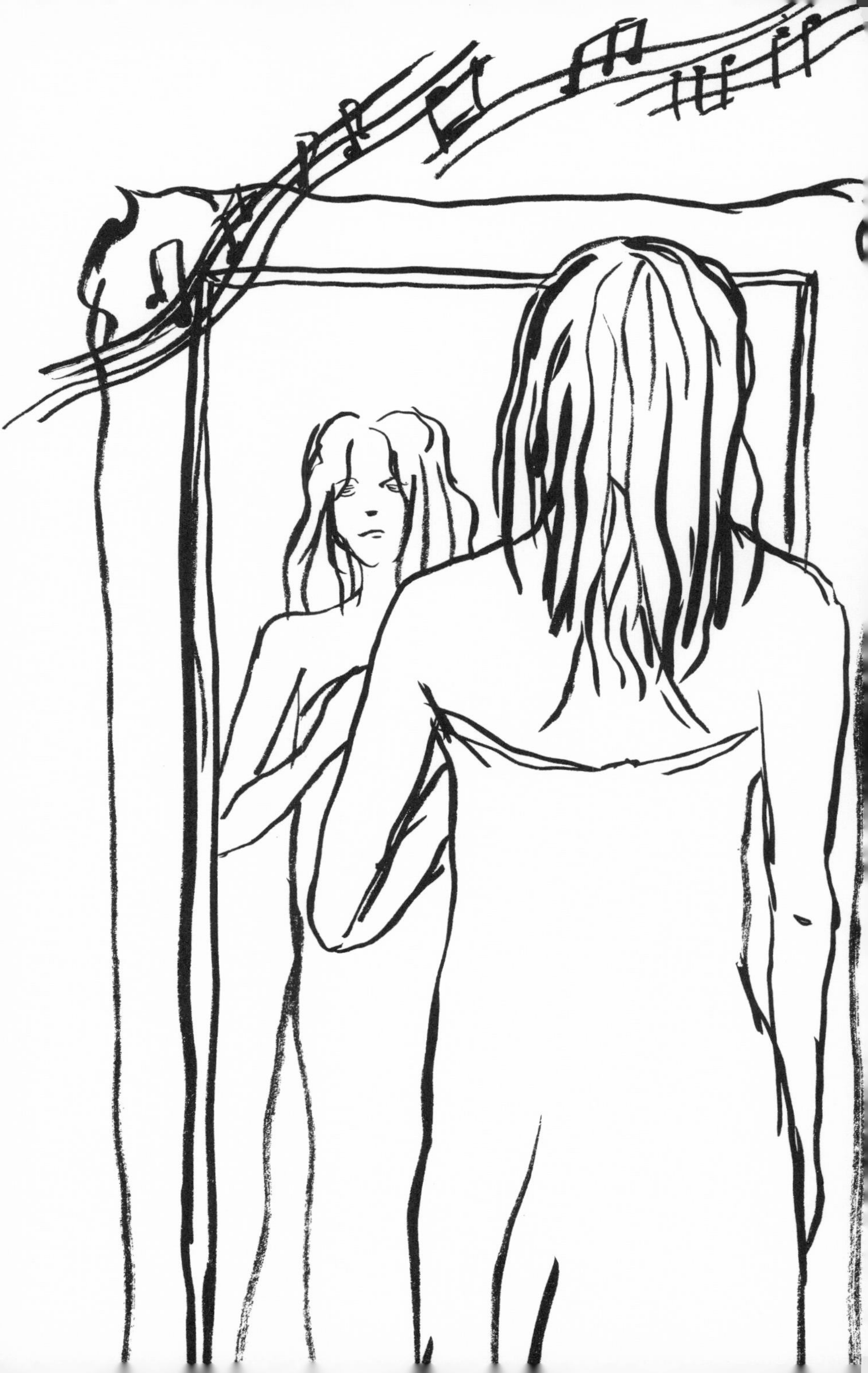

Mimi and Evan grew up in the same neighborhood. A year into dating him, Mimi found out that it was Evan's ex-girlfriend Cindy who had tried to strangle her in the schoolyard when Mimi was eight.

Brian's ex-girlfriend was much older. Her name was Lena and she had three grown children. She spoke slowly, with a deep Russian accent.

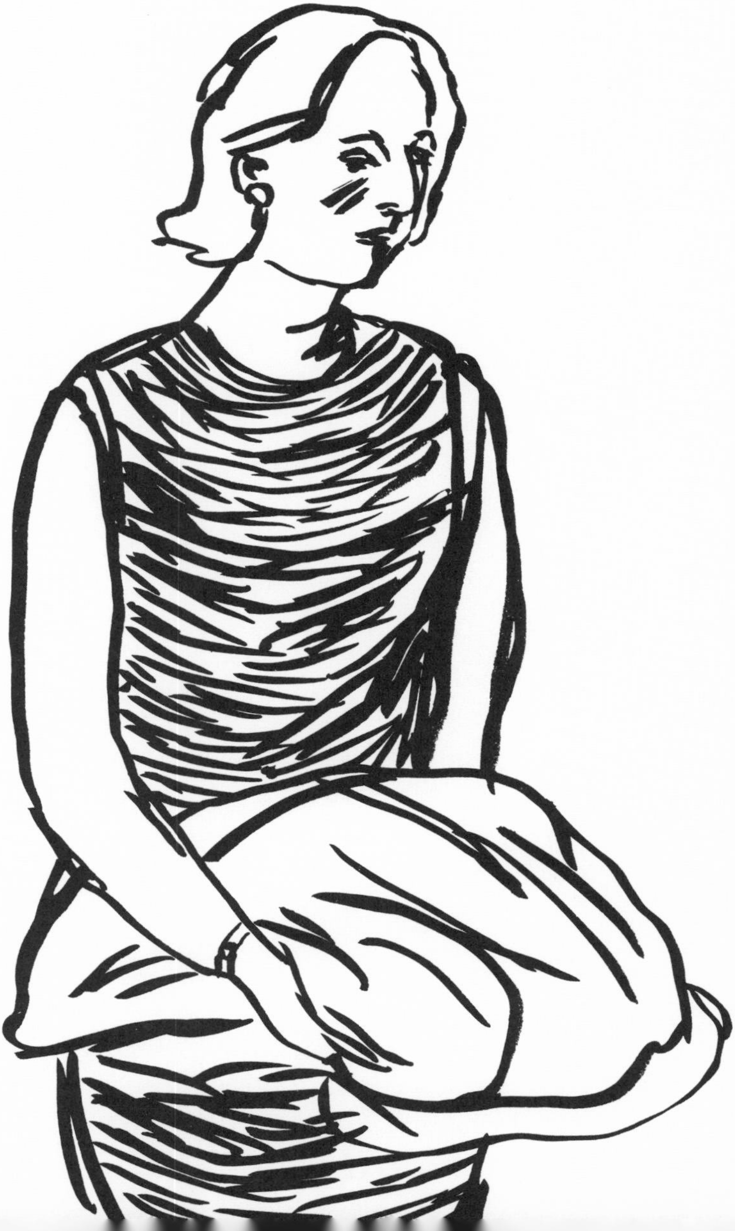

Lena's ex-boyfriend Paul made much less money than her other boyfriends. She loved him the best, but he always felt he had something to prove.

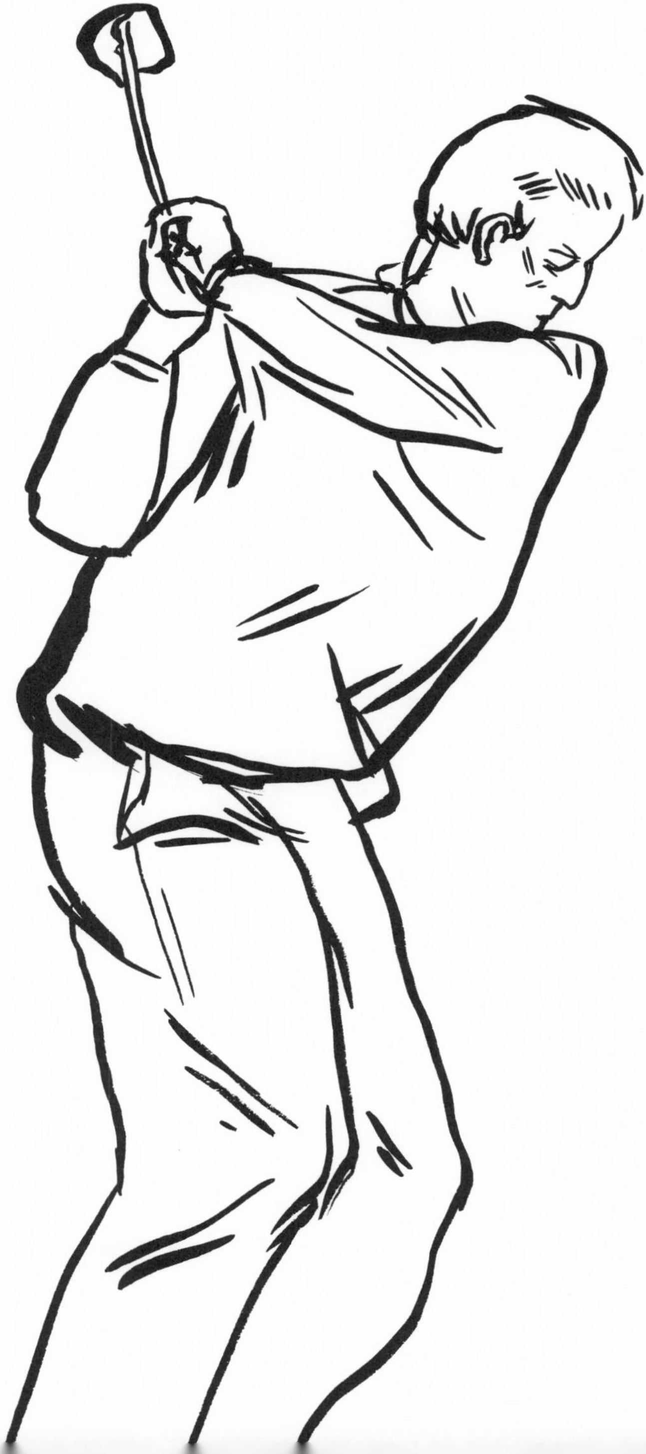

Joe kept a photograph of his ex-girlfriend in a frame on top of his upright piano. One day his girlfriend Stacy felt like dusting and the photograph accidentally fell between the piano and the wall.

Isabelle found a vacation snapshot of her boyfriend's ex-girlfriend. She ripped it up and left it in a neat pile on his pillow.

Claudine had a small emergency in the middle of a romantic dinner at her new boyfriend's apartment. To her relief and equally her dismay, she found half a box of tampons in the medicine cabinet.

Jeff's ex-girlfriend Monica was from Trieste. Julie looked it up on a map to see where it was.

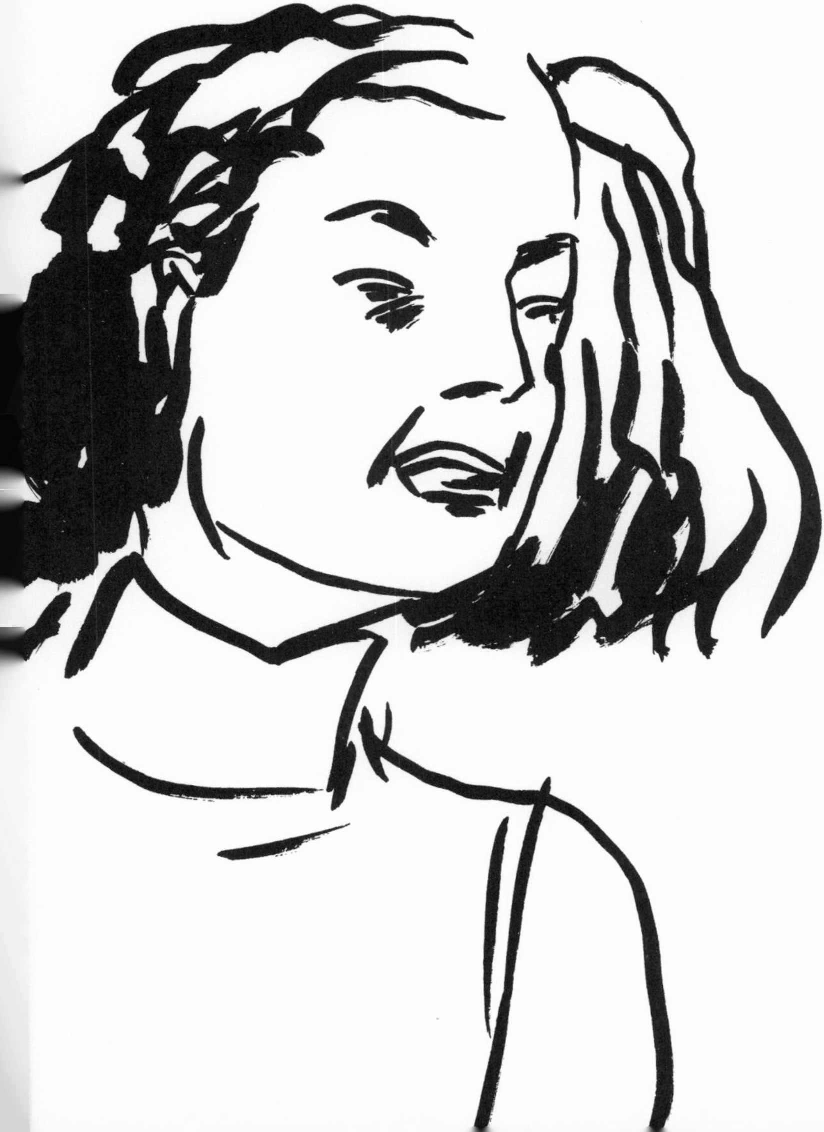

When Monica arrived from Italy to visit Jeff, he asked Julie for some space. Julie left fourteen identical messages on Jeff's machine. She asked, "Have you told her about me yet?" and then hung up.

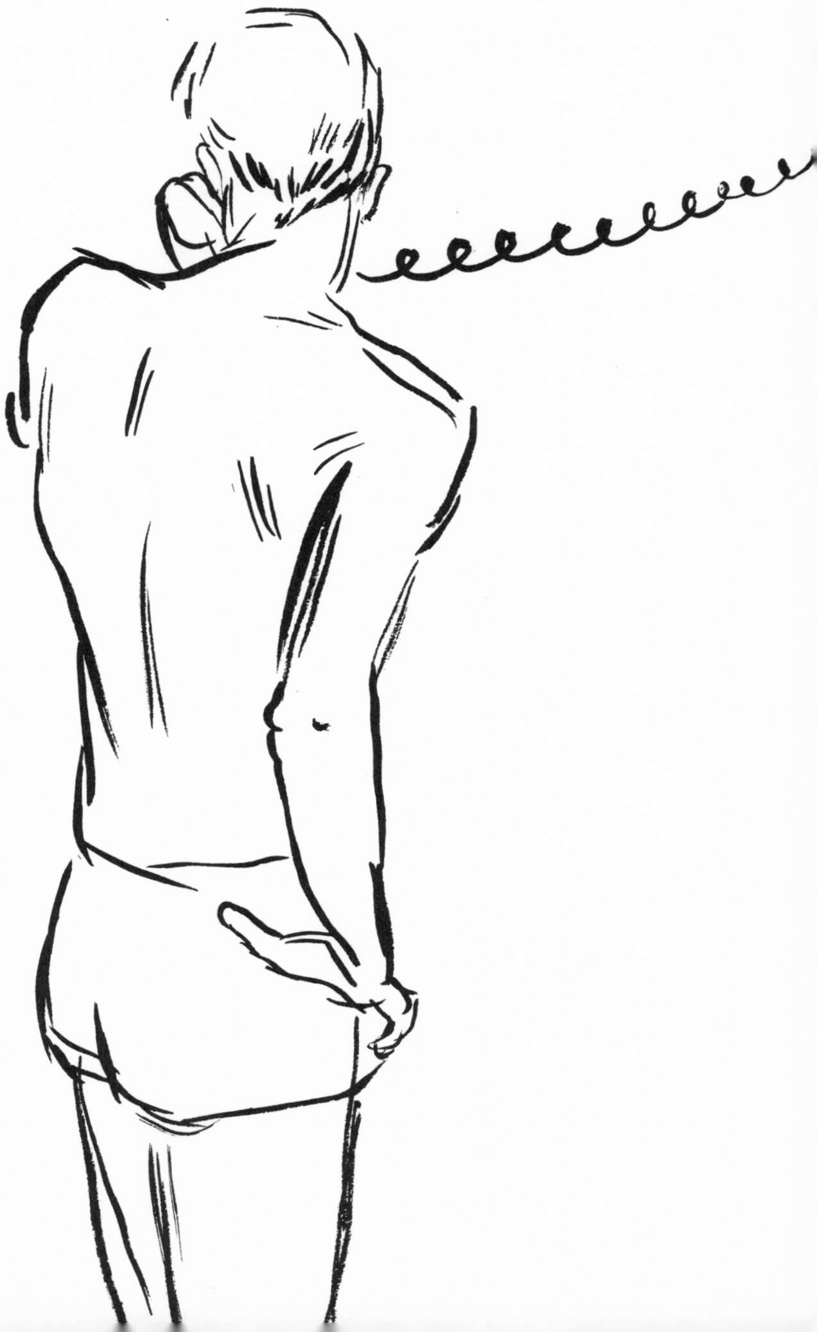

Alec's ex-girlfriend Renata was an heiress with a thing for father figures.

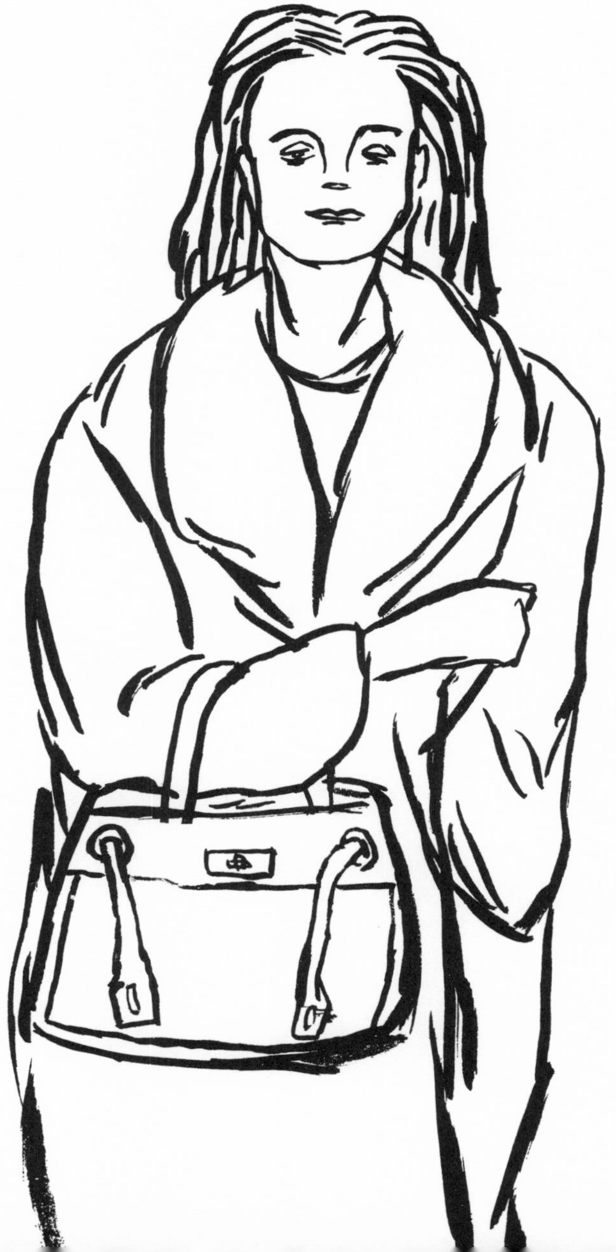

Bobby's ex-girlfriend Nina was a gifted but troubled singer. She would constantly cancel shows due to crippling stage fright. Her career suffered, but her rare records are critically acclaimed and in high demand among musicians.

She wrote a lot of songs about her and Bobby.

Ted's ex-girlfriend was a fashion designer.

Elizabeth had no problem with exes. It was the women who replaced her that drove her crazy. They always had:

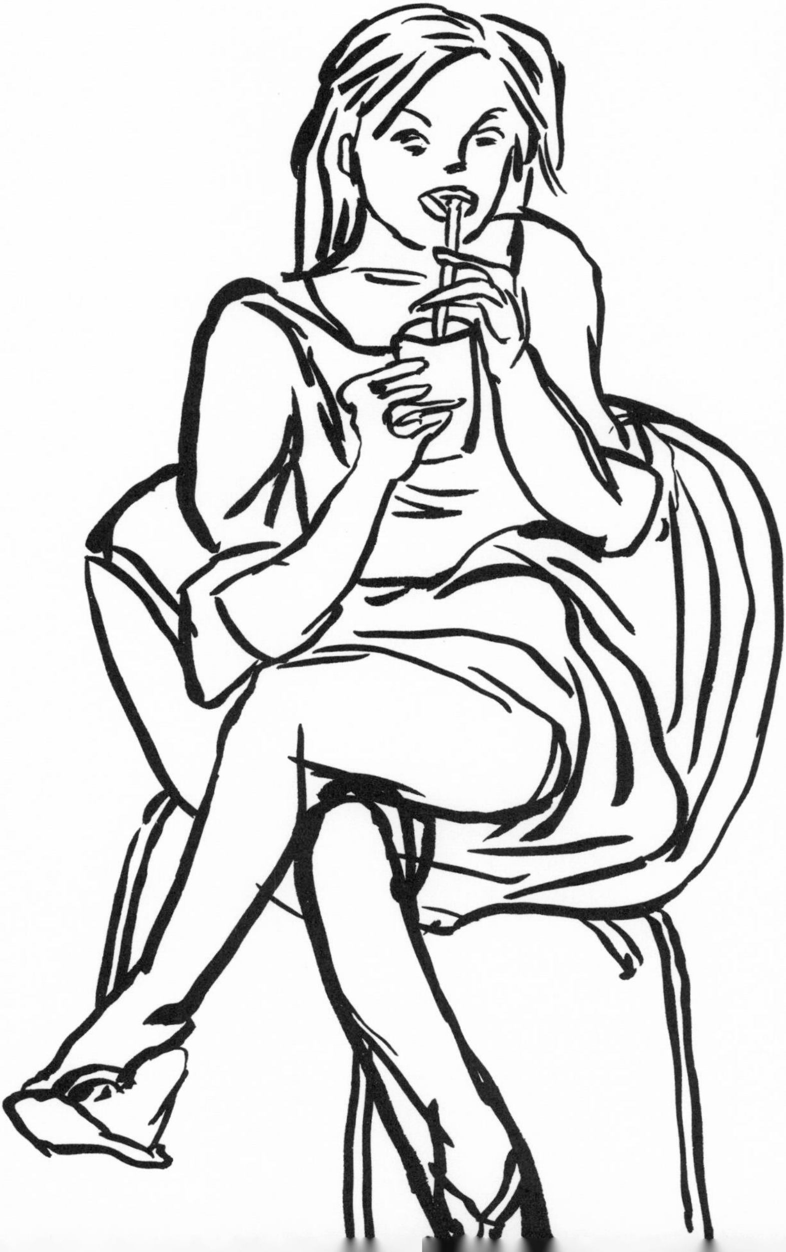

thinner ankles,

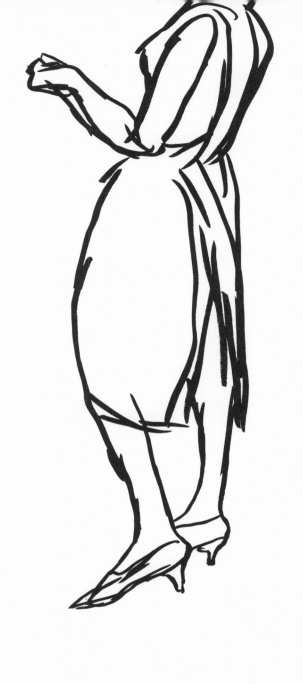

poutier lips,

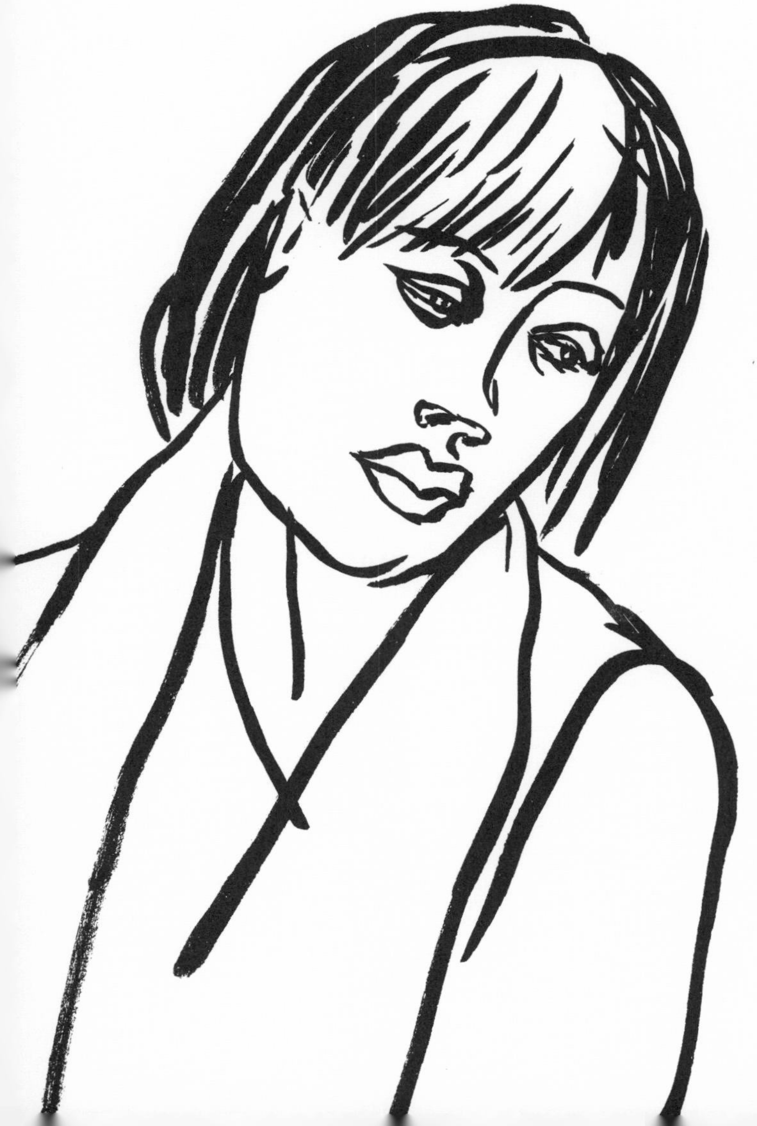

and PhDs.

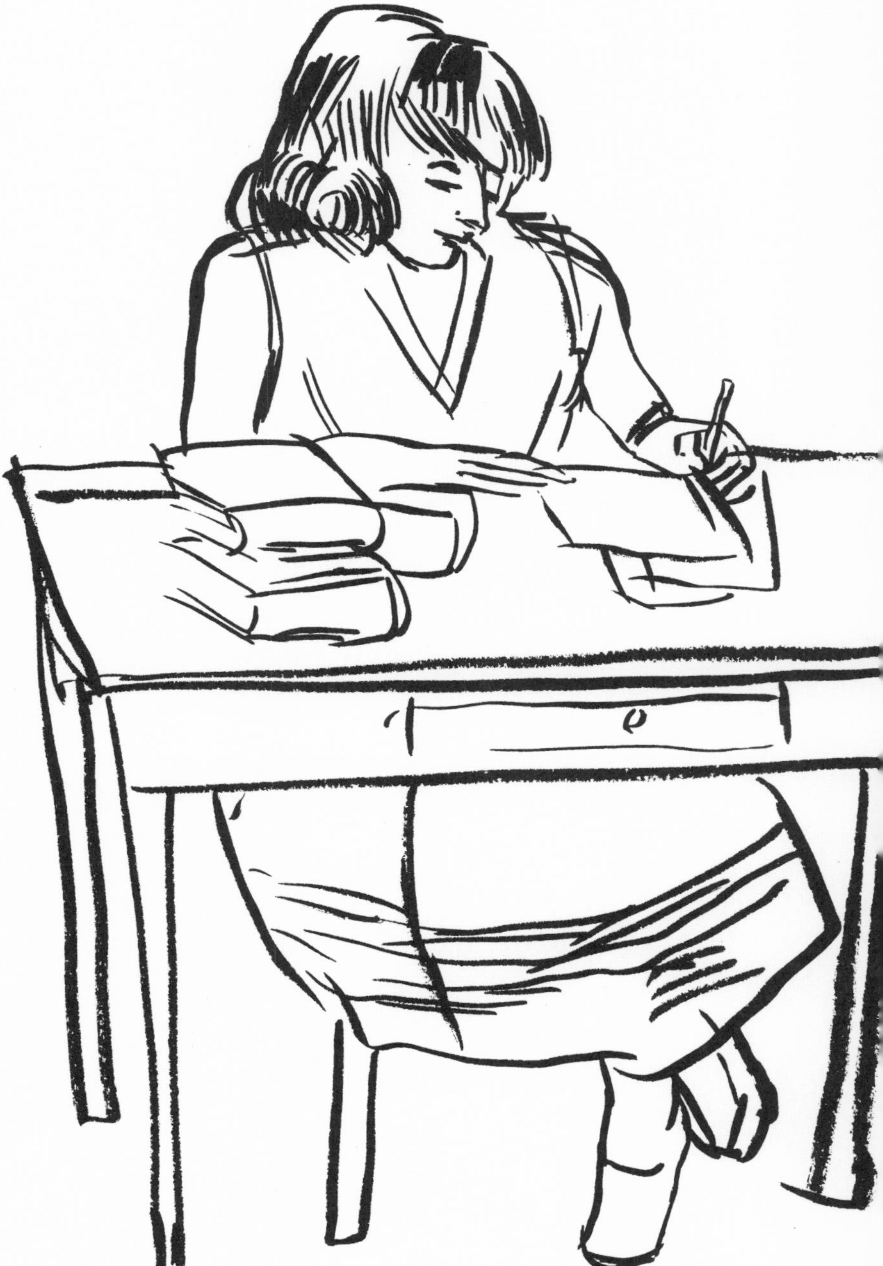

Fred's ex-girlfriend Ghislaine was muse to
the chief designer at a centuries-old fashion house.
He said she was clairvoyant. She was bisexual.

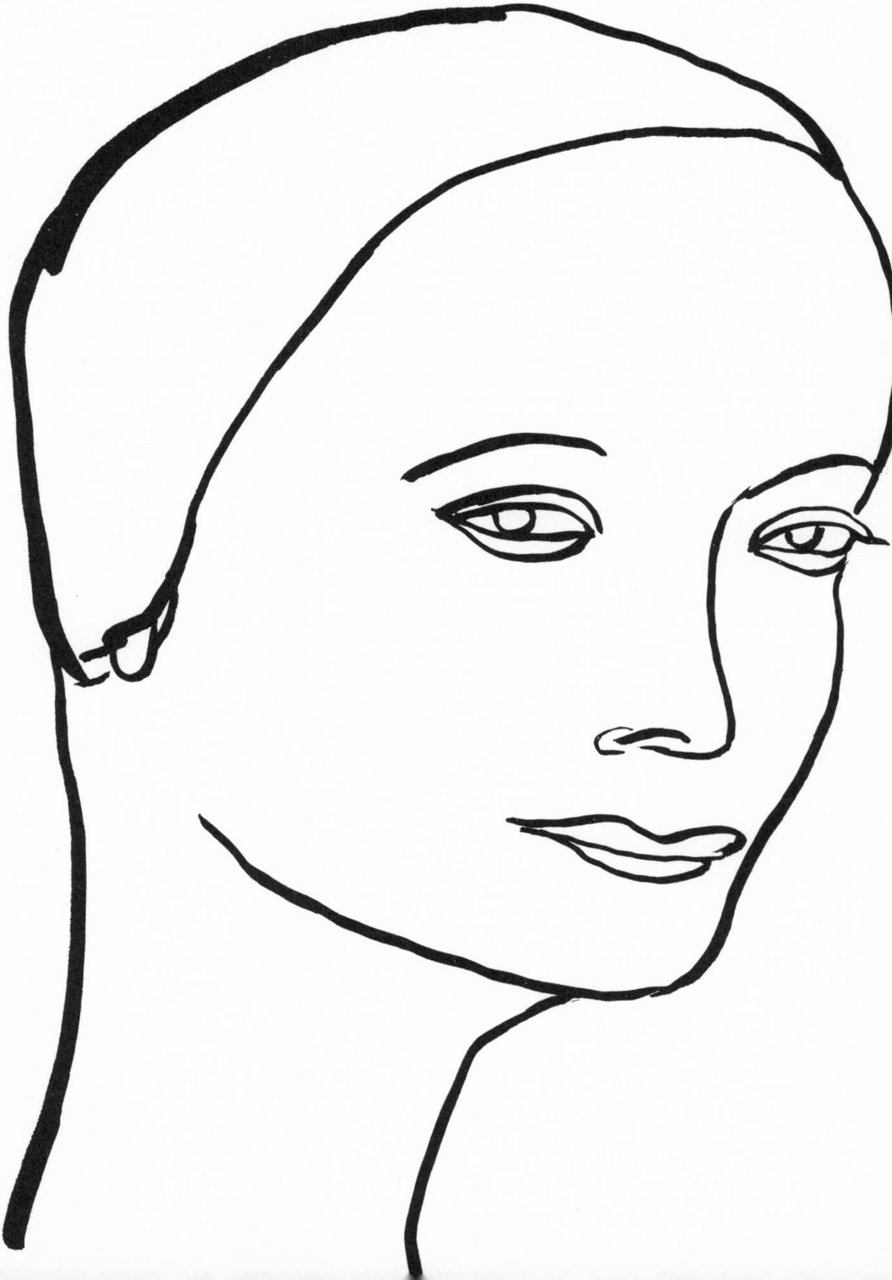

Ghislaine's ex-girlfriend Sophie borrowed a lot of her clothes, but never reciprocated. Eventually Ghislaine became resentful of this.

Todd's ex-girlfriend Wendy had sexy moles on interesting parts of her body.

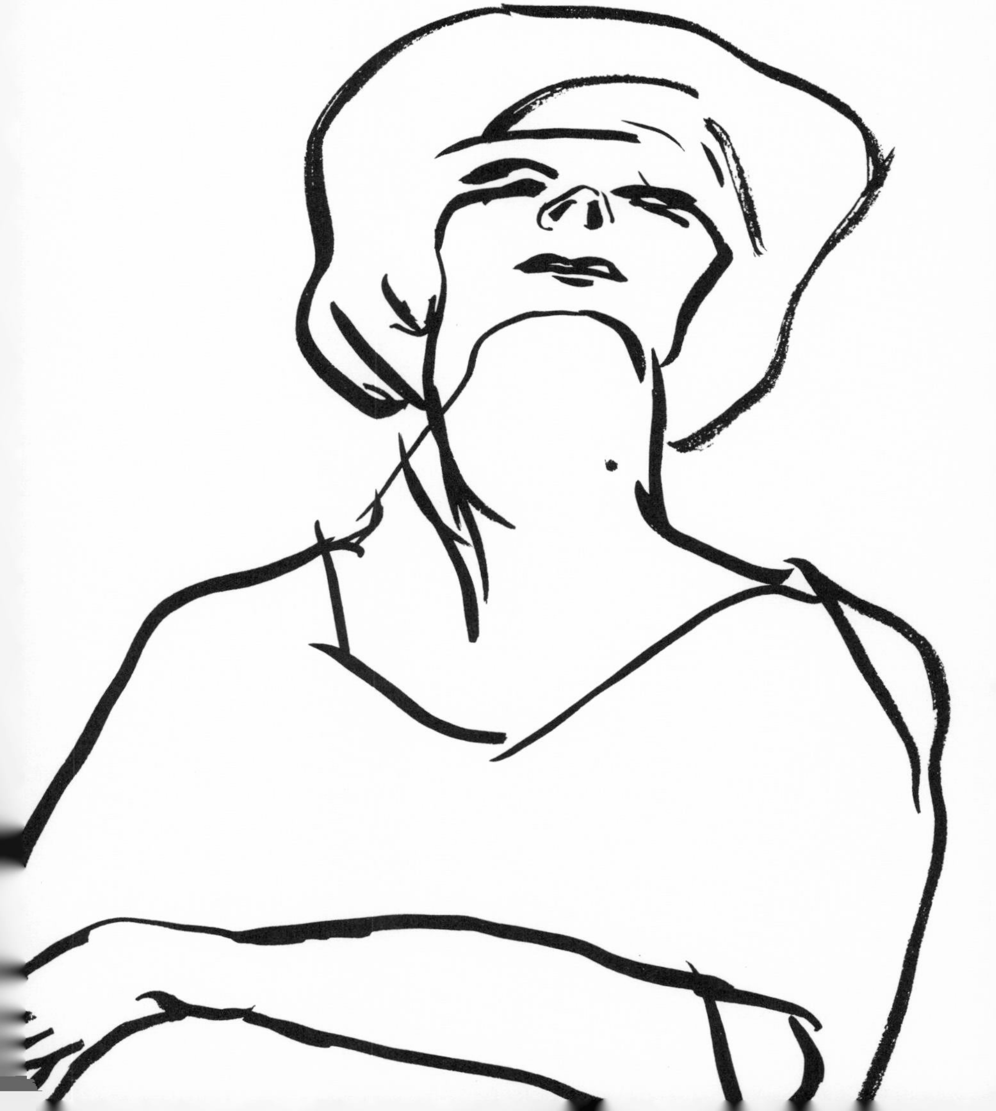

Isaac would not let Rebecca answer the telephone in his apartment.

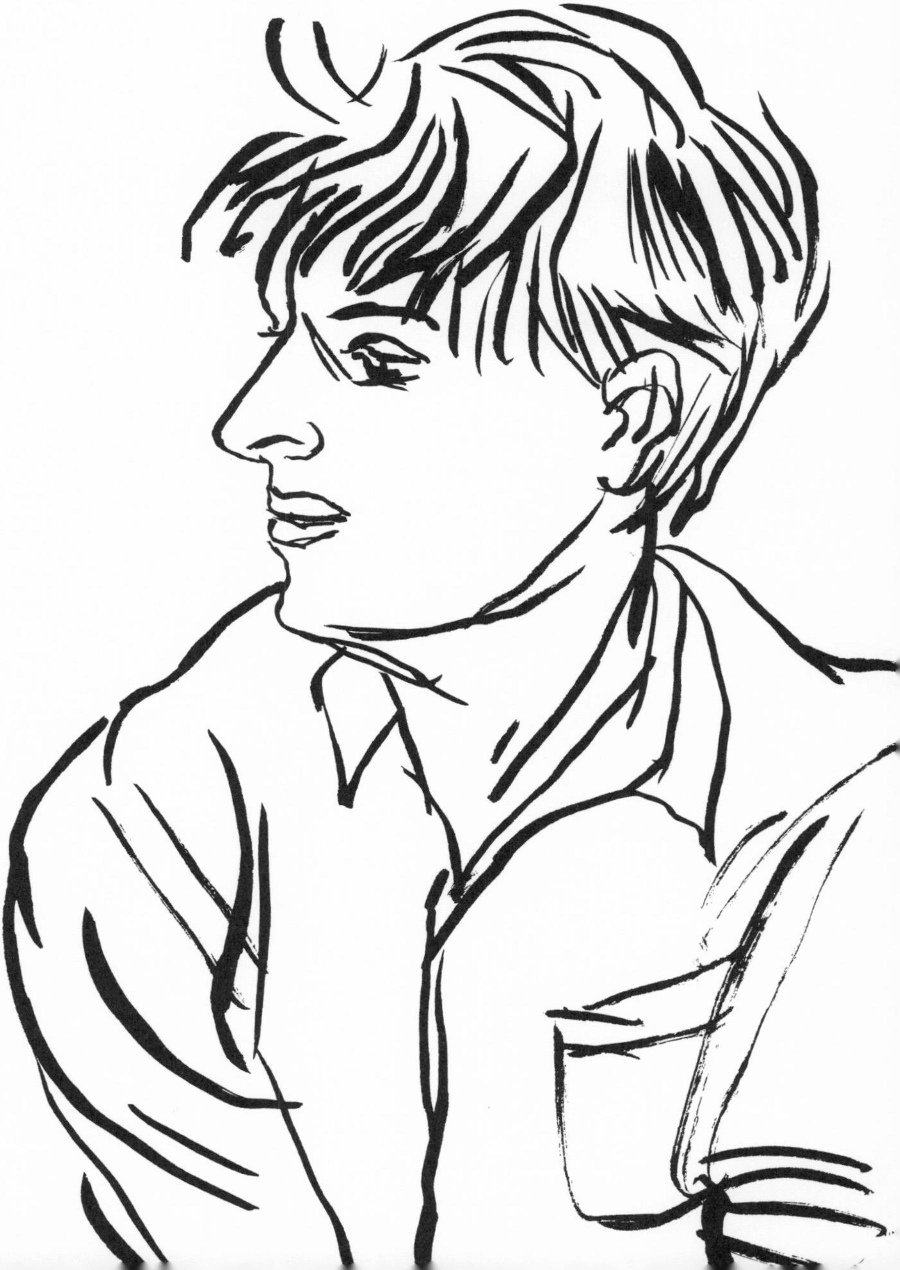

Norman's ex-girlfriend Agnes was a persuasive and graceful salesperson. She wore a subtle but intoxicating perfume, a mix she made herself from Fracas, vetiver essential oil, and Old Spice.

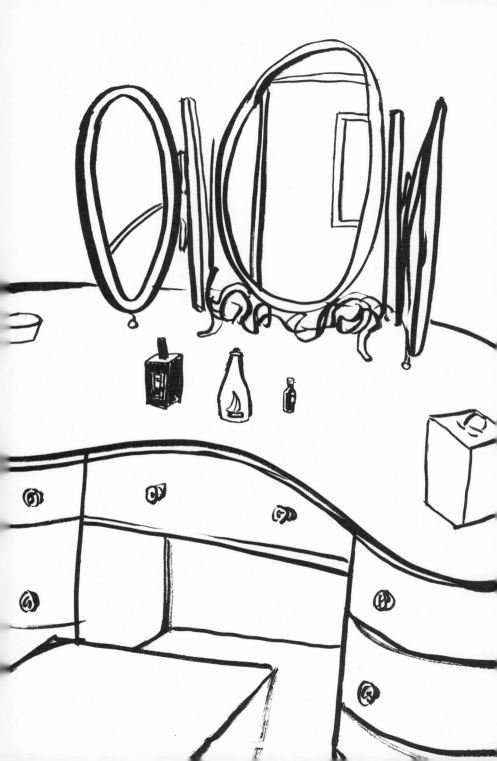

Owen was Agnes's ex-boyfriend. He had introduced her as his "friend" one too many times.

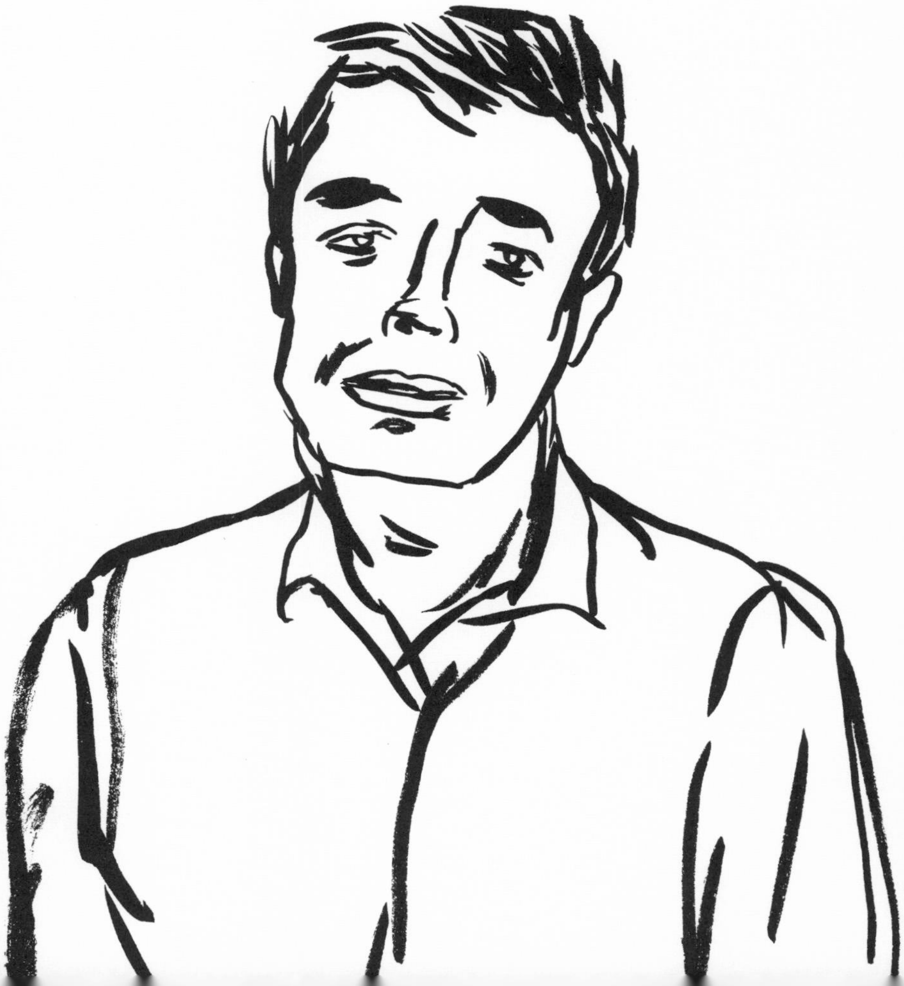

Sarah was Michael's ex-girlfriend for ten years, but would eventually be his wife.

Philip's ex-girlfriend Estefania was an aggressive Argentinian supermodel and the face of a multinational cosmetics conglomerate. Philip would point out her picture to his girlfriend in magazine advertisements and on display in airport duty-free shops.

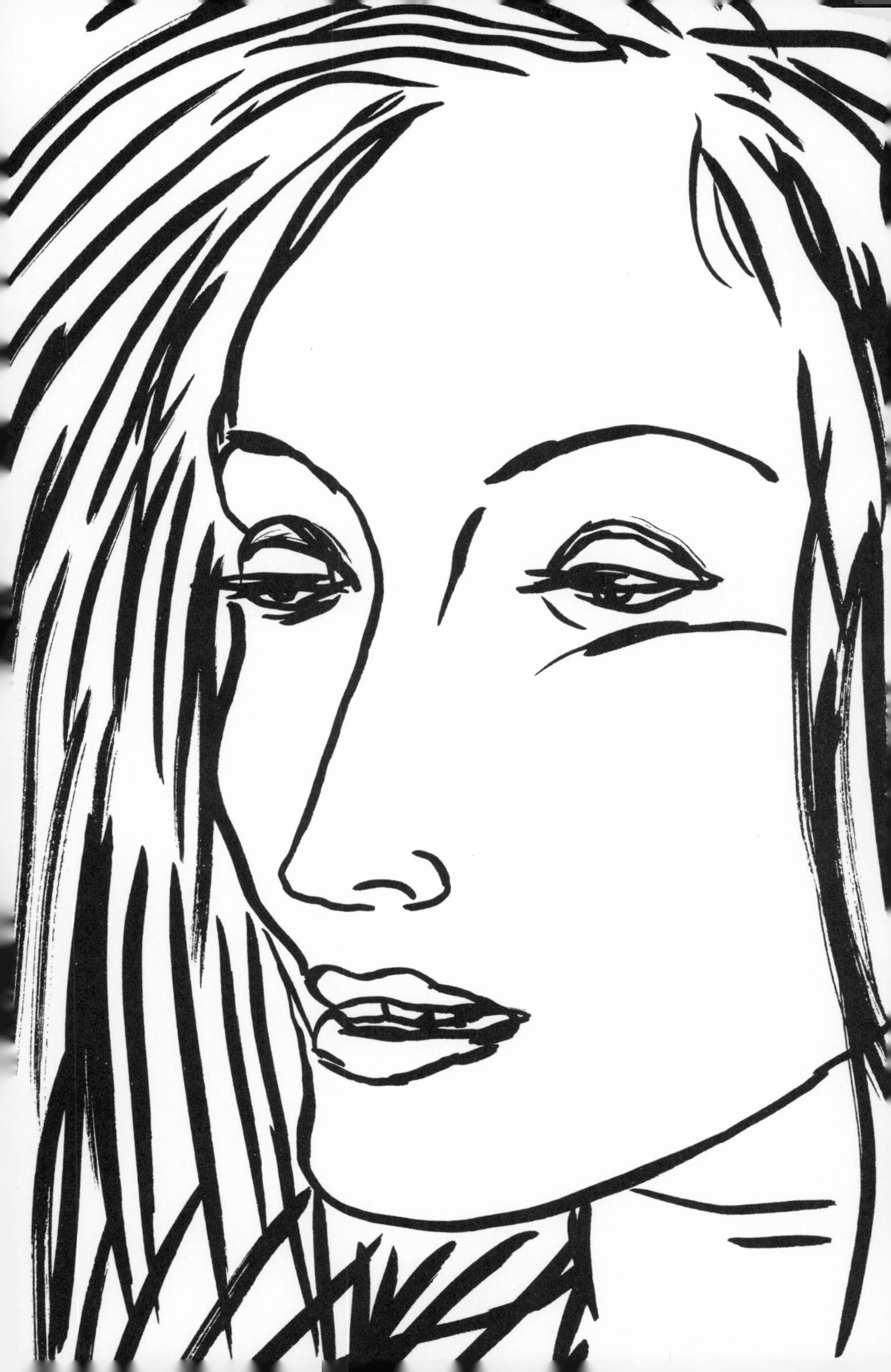

Estefania's ex-boyfriend suggested she wear darker jeans.

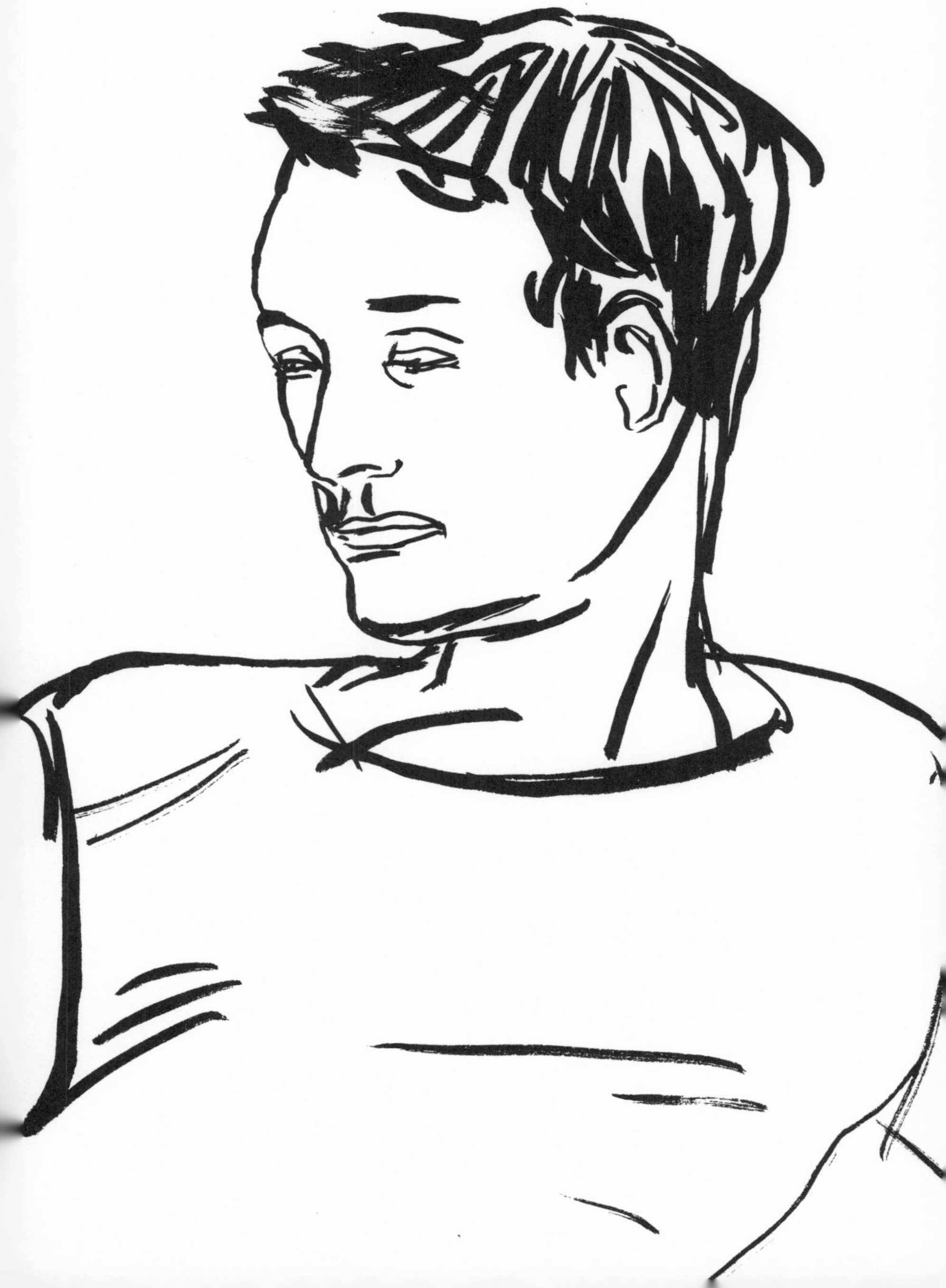

Carl's ex-girlfriend was Sheila. They'd had a heavy relationship in high school and made sure they kept in touch throughout their lives. They sometimes find themselves in the same Midwestern city for business.

Ken's ex-girlfriend Sonya had been wearing
Japanese designer clothes for decades.

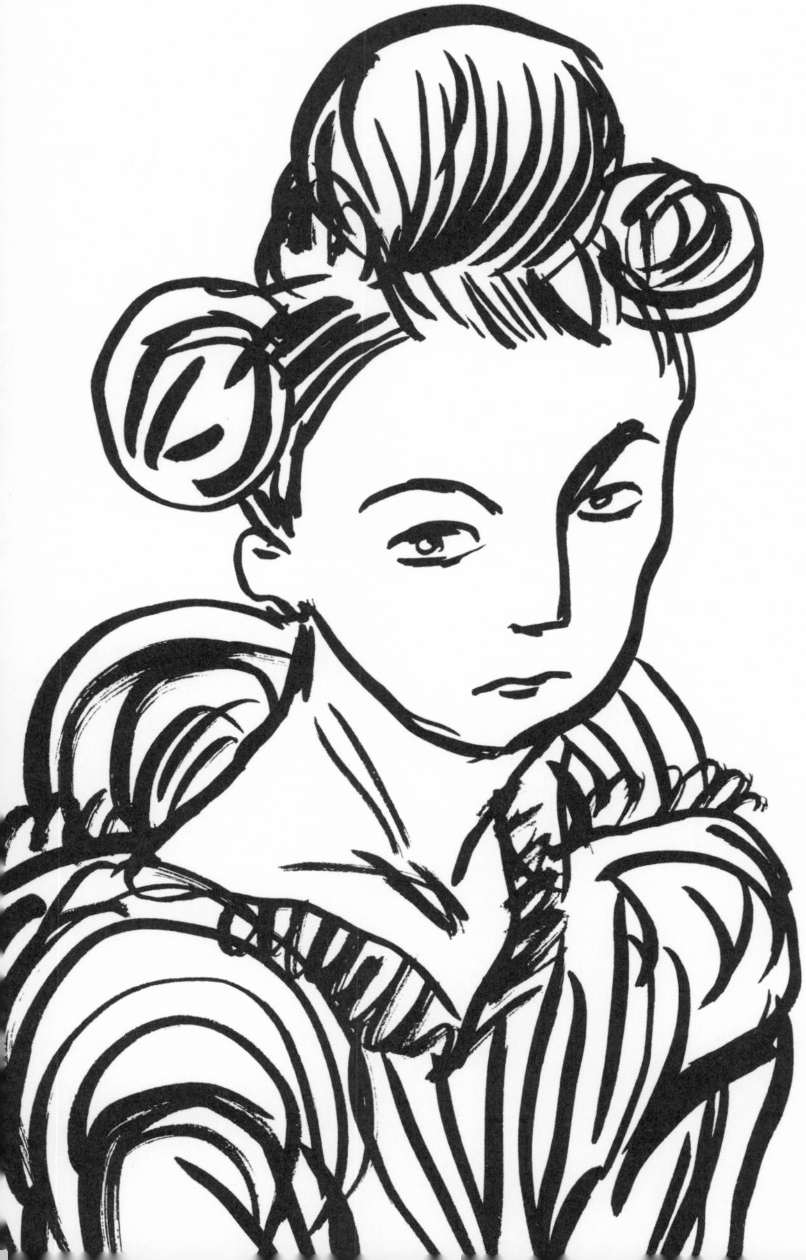

Sonya's ex-boyfriend Akira was a fine-art photographer. He published a book of photographs, all of them intimate portraits of Sonya taken during the lean years they had spent together in Japan.

Jean-Paul's ex-girlfriend Eugénie could soft-boil
an egg, make fresh coffee, and toast a baguette all
in the time it took her to roll a cigarette, light it over
the gas flame, and smoke it patiently at the stove
in her underwear. She did this after rising late
each morning.

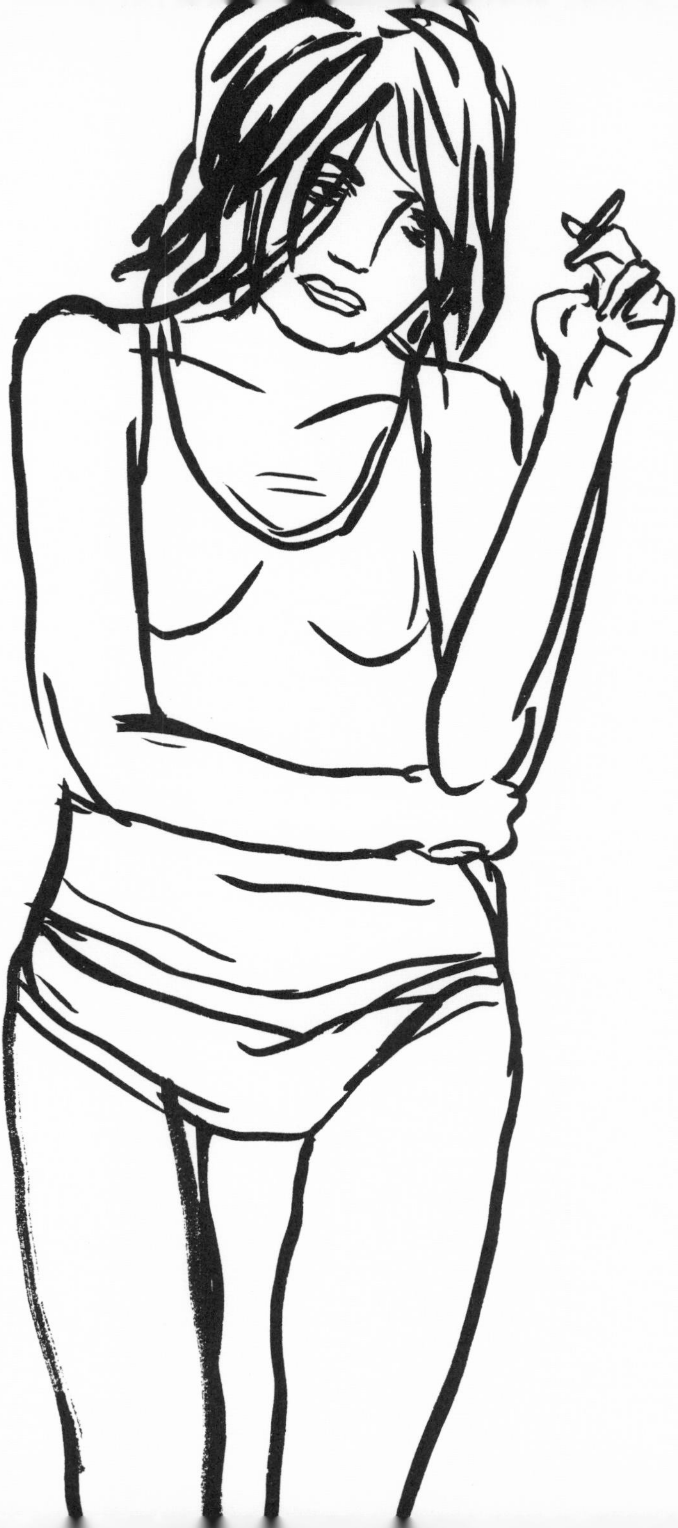

When Eugénie moved in with Stuart, she came across a woman's winter coat in his closet. She asked him how long it had been there, and he said about a year. She asked him whose it was, and he said it belonged to his ex-girlfriend and he was just keeping it in case she wanted it back.

Eugénie also found a hair clip. She threw it in the garbage.

There was a vase in the dining room that didn't quite seem to Stuart's taste. Eugénie couldn't throw it away, so she hid it in a cabinet.

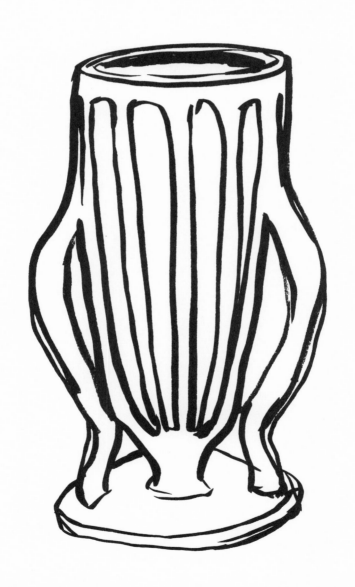

Alan's ex-girlfriend Adrienne was not his ex-girlfriend. She was his girlfriend.

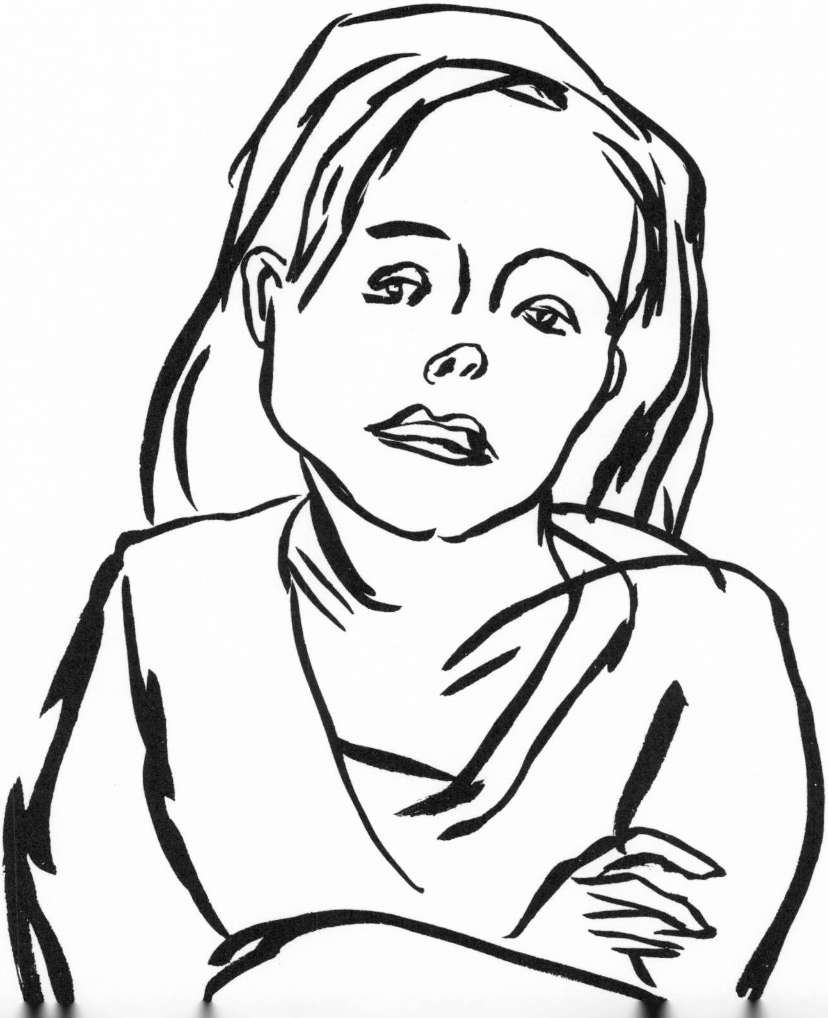

Shane's ex-girlfriend was a child prodigy.

Lionel's ex-girlfriend Edie enjoyed Brahms.
But she preferred money.

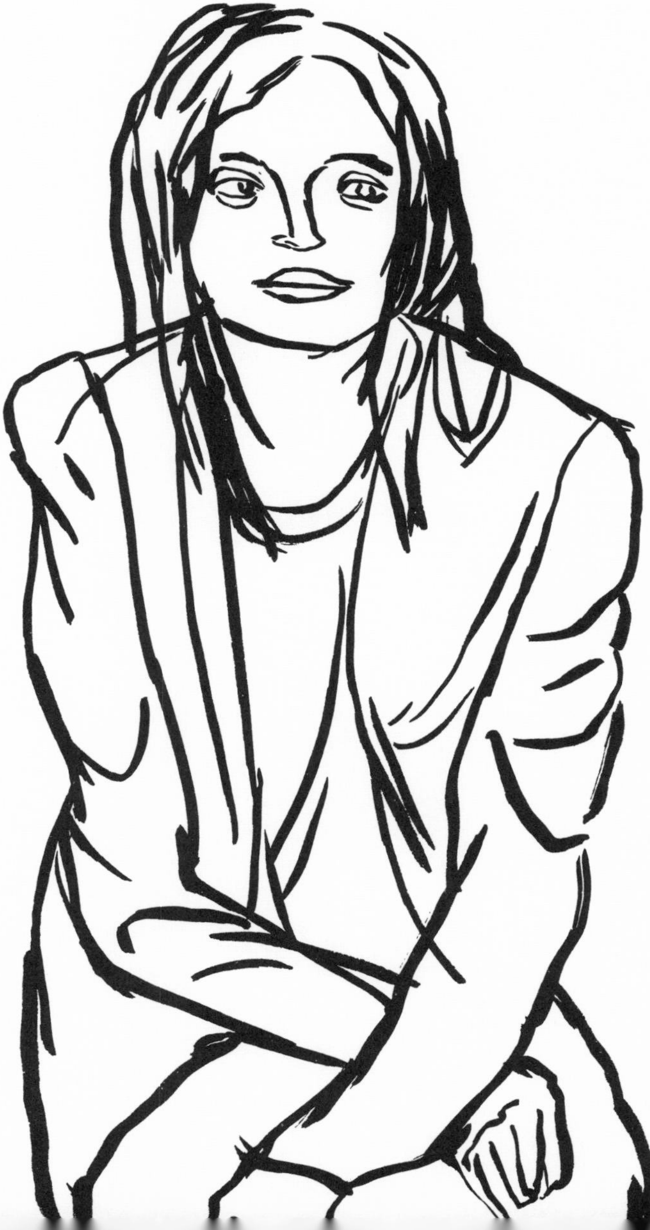

Tanya's ex-boyfriend Marcel once told her that the sex they had was "up there with the best."

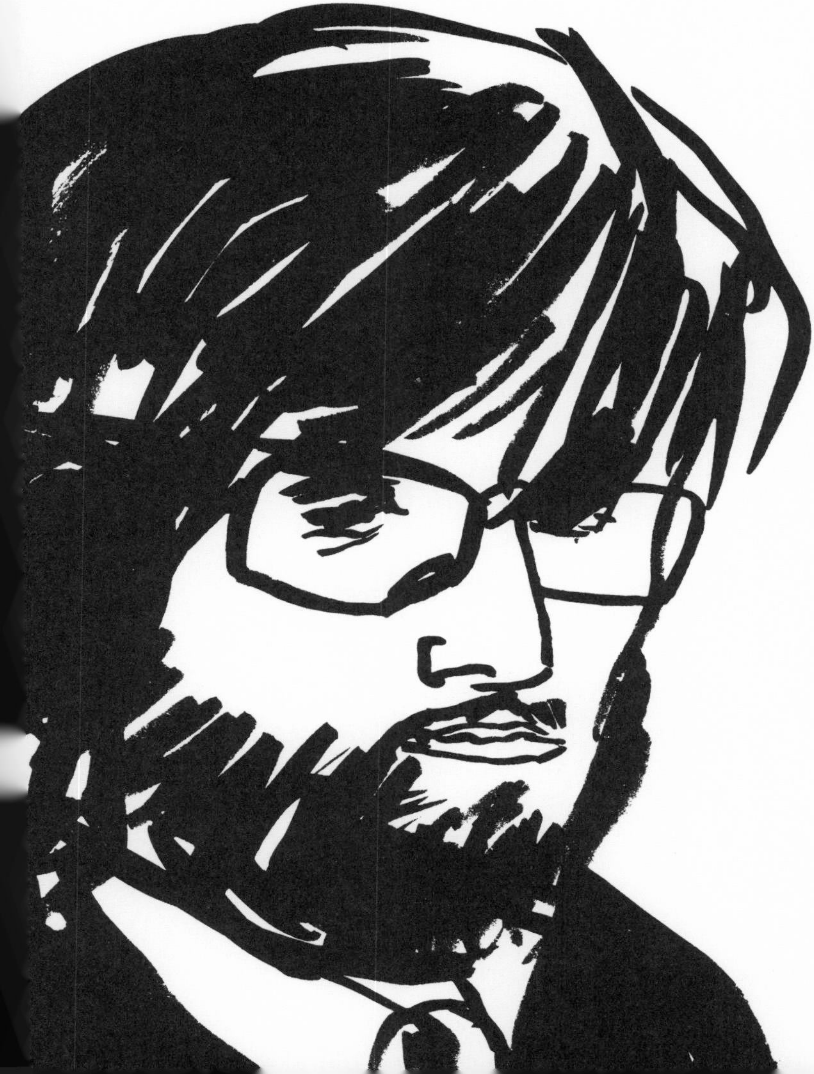

When Tanya told her best friend, Rita, Rita
confided that she was once told by her ex-boyfriend
Bjorn that the sex they had was the most "loving"
sex he'd experienced. Unsure whether this was a
compliment, Rita had pressed him further. Bjorn
then admitted to having "spicy" but not "loving"
sex with his ex-girlfriend Yael.

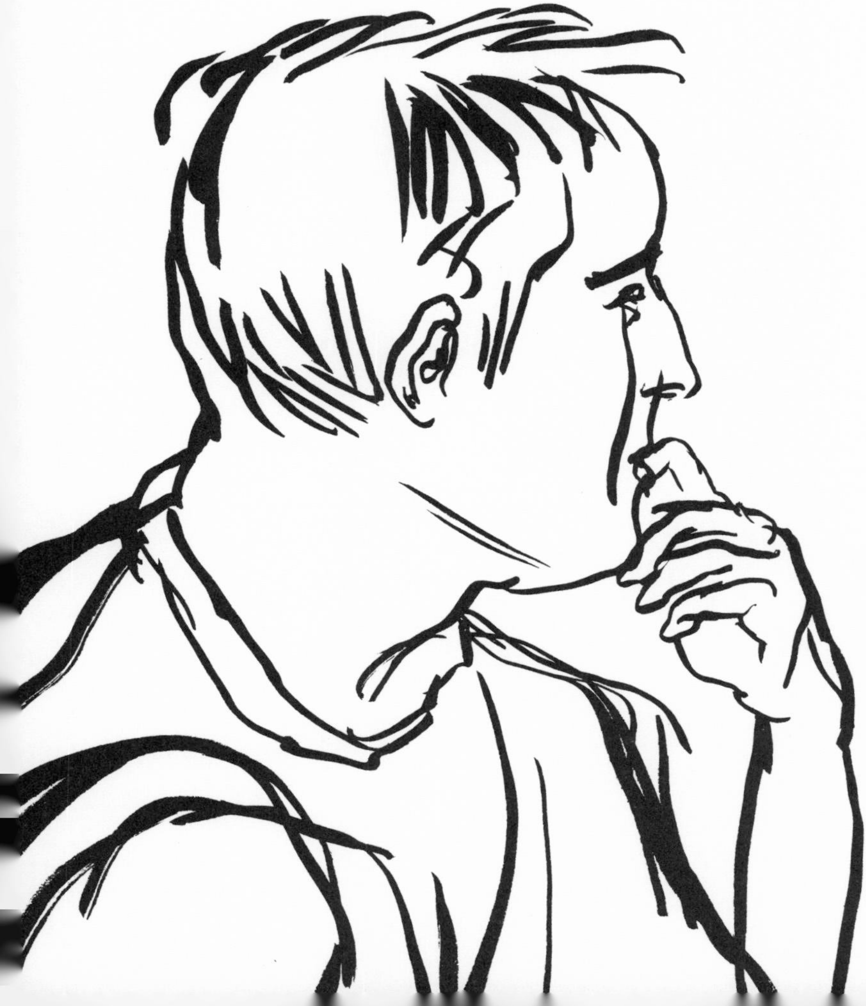

Lewis's ex-girlfriend's name—Fiona—came up at dinner one night. There was silence between Lewis and his girlfriend, Judy, for eleven minutes as they cut and chewed their steaks.

FIONA

FIONA

Harvey was a theater director who preferred to date black women. Harvey's girlfriend, Olivia, was constantly correcting his producers, crews, and cast as they greeted or introduced her as "Karen," Harvey's previous girlfriend.

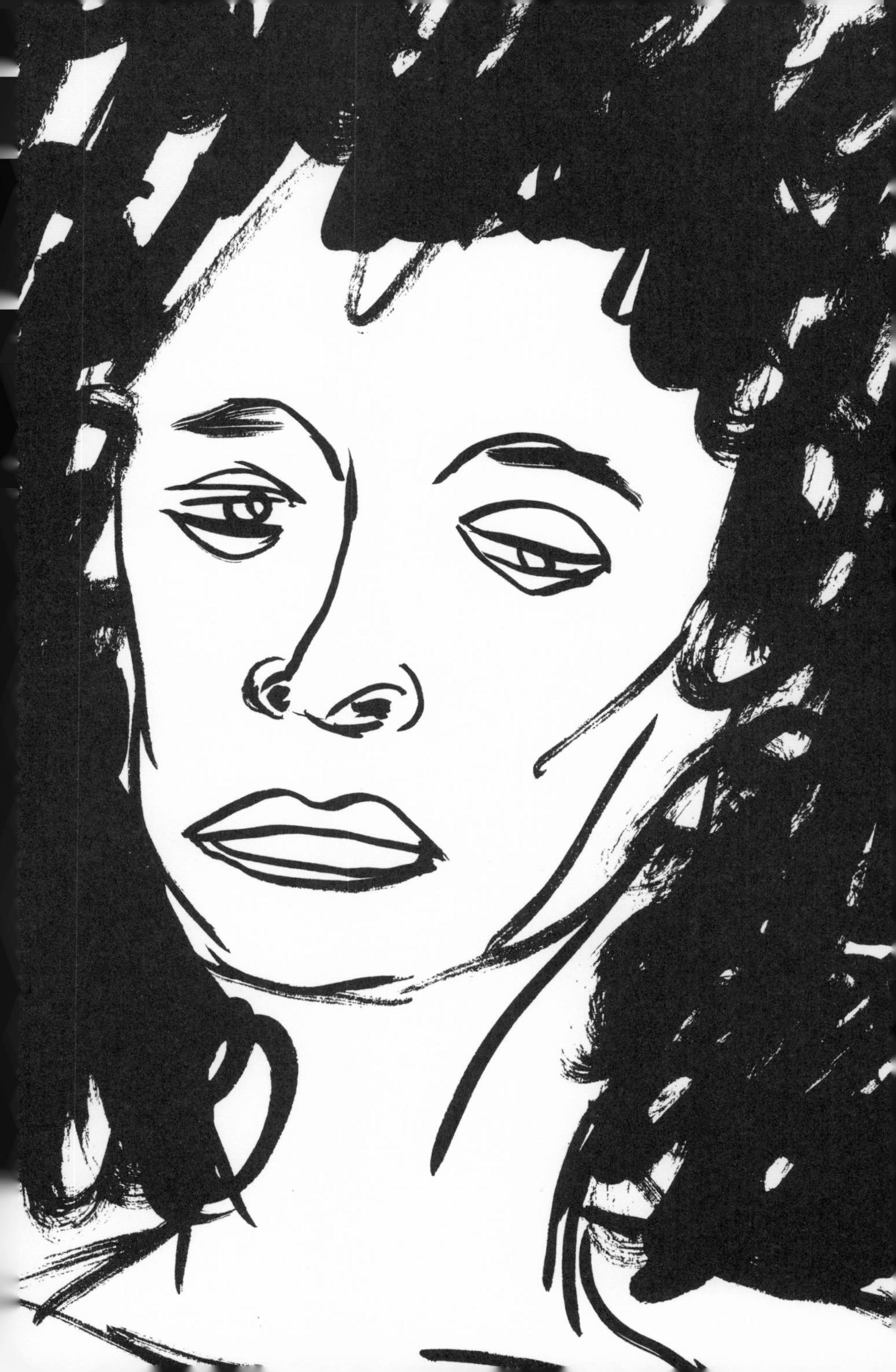

When Elinor began dating Quentin, she found a lovingly inscribed copy of *The Reluctant Submissive's Handbook* placed backwards on the bookshelf.

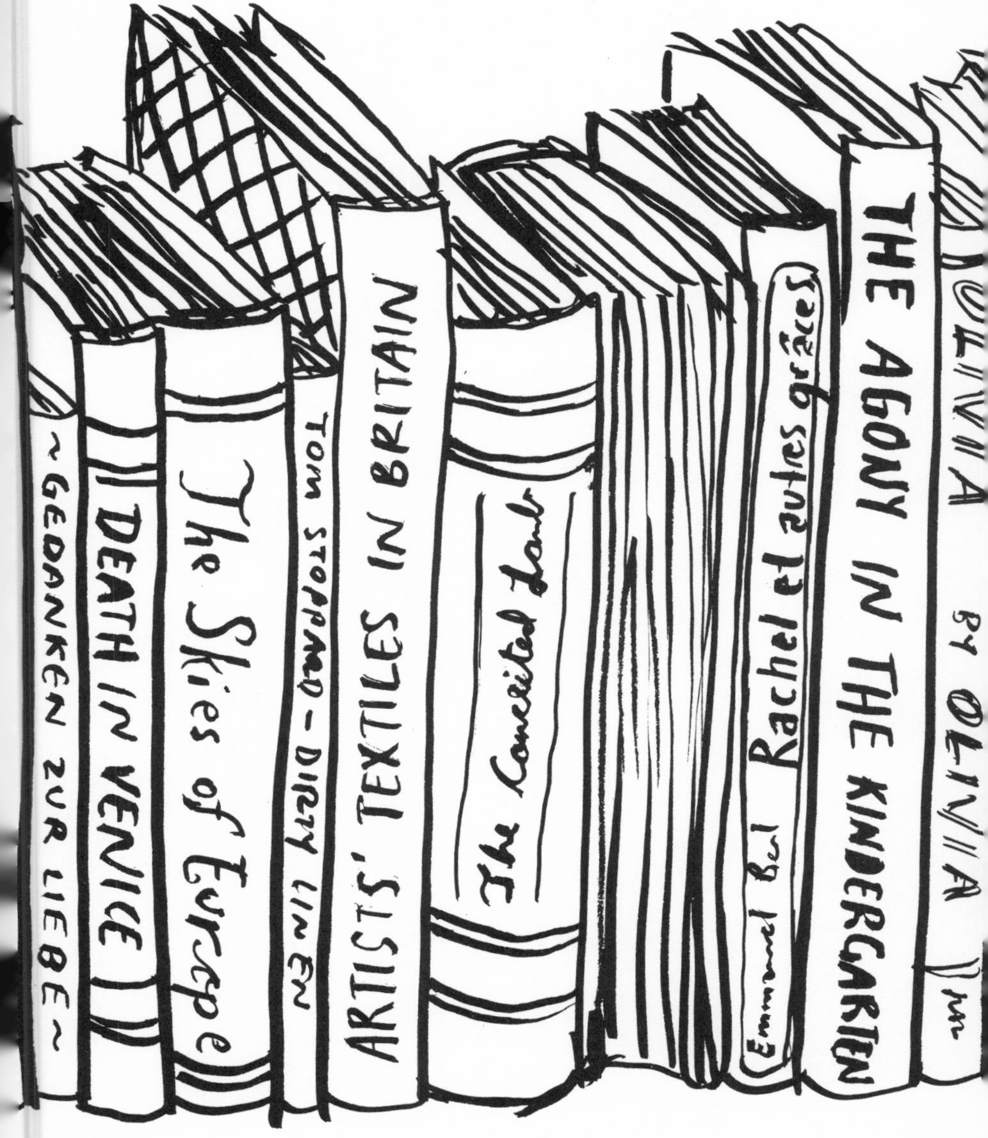
~GEDANKEN ZUR LIEBE~
DEATH IN VENICE
The Skies of Europe
TOM STOPPARD - DIRTY LINEN
ARTISTS' TEXTILES IN BRITAIN
The Conceited Lamb
Emmanuel Bove
Rachel et autres grâces
THE AGONY IN THE KINDERGARTEN
OLIVIA BY OLIVIA

Eric's ex-girlfriend was Joanna. She has since married, but every few years sends Eric letters with no return address, expressing how fondly she remembers their time together.

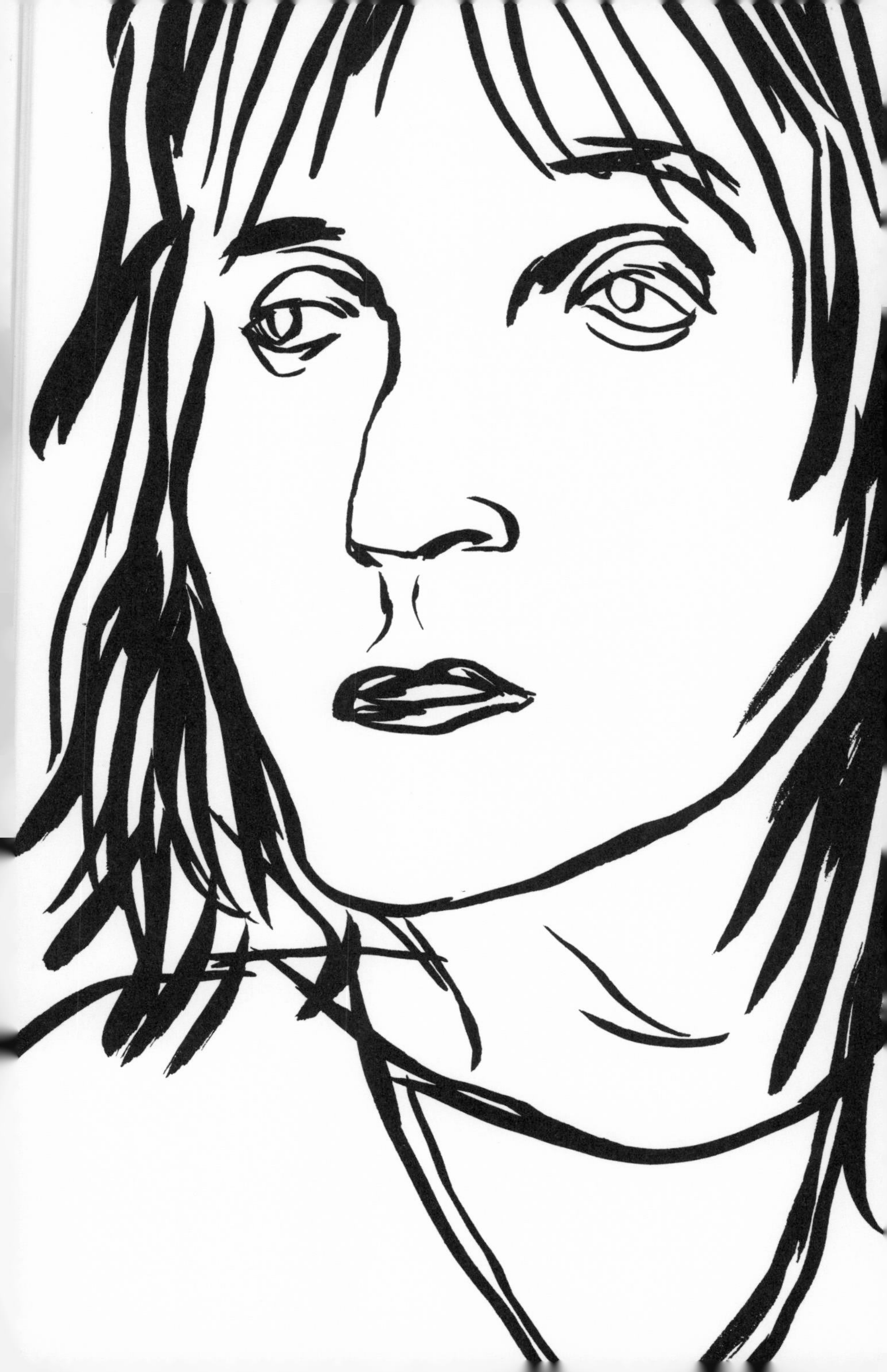

Milosz scrupulously updates his address book with his ex-girlfriend's current numbers, even if he hasn't spoken to them in years.

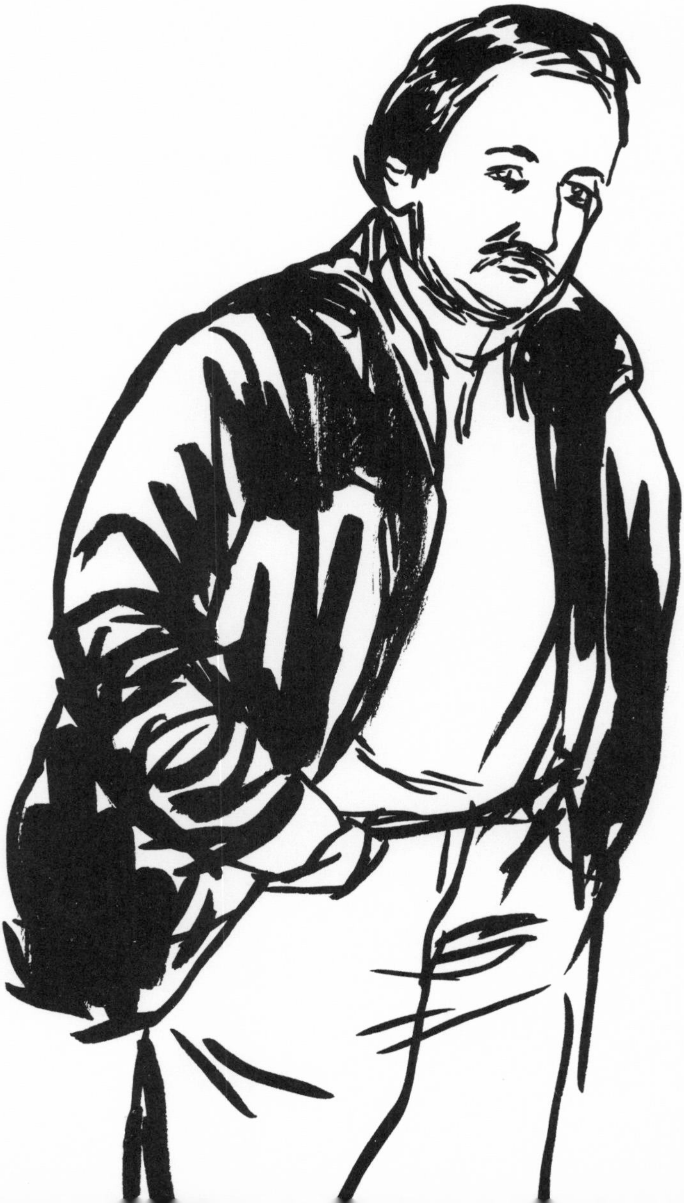

Margaret came across a box of old journals belonging to her boyfriend, Scott. She couldn't help herself from skimming a few pages.

In them Margaret found detailed and heartfelt entries about women Scott had dated well before she met him. Some he had loved deeply, some he had not; some Scott had told Margaret about, some he had not.

One entry described the day he met Jan, the walk they took across the snowy campus, and the intimate and exhilarating conversation they had. There were entries about their shared love of Welsh rarebit, lists of the books they had lent each other, and the anxiousness he felt about her feelings toward him.

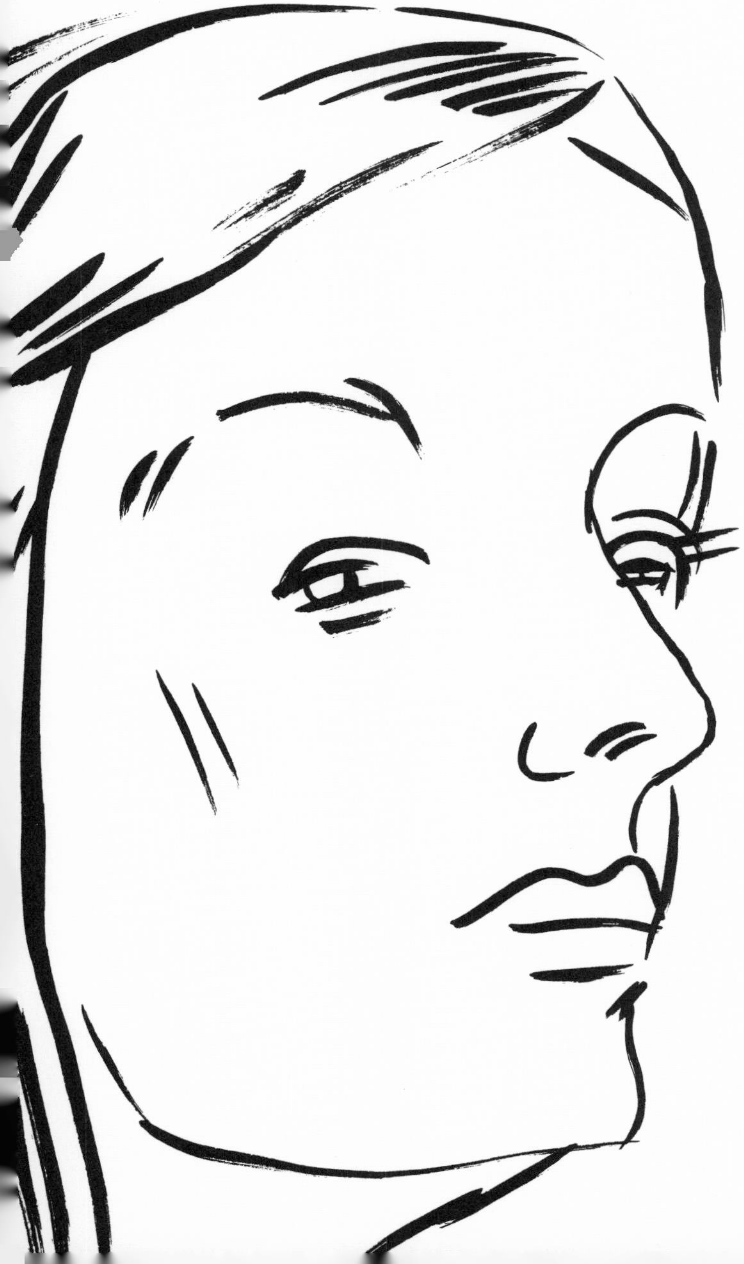

There was April, a divorcée Scott saw whenever he was in Chicago.

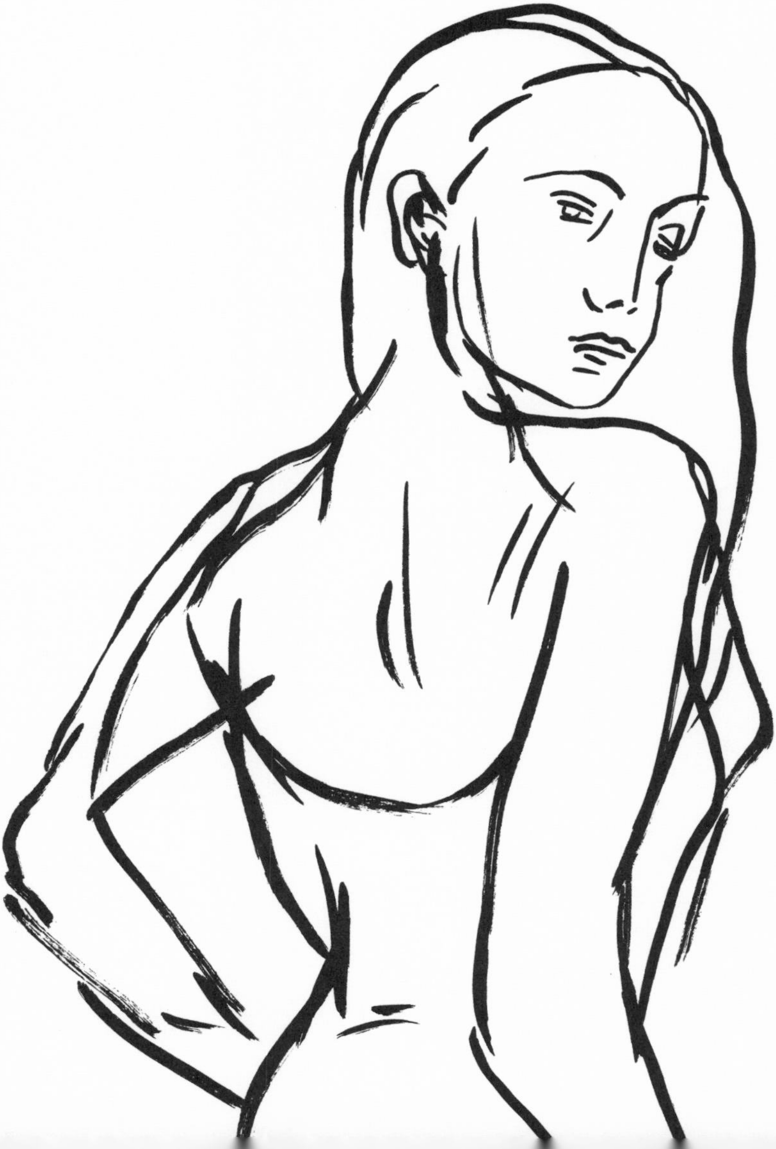

Margaret noticed various entries about Helen, who was always involved while she saw Scott, but with whom Scott began to vividly imagine a life.

Another page described the sex he had with Sheryl, the fruitlessness of their relationship (rebounds, both), but the intense attraction of the games they played.

Scott described seeing Greta on the subway with
another man, and feeling jealous, but sorry
for the man.

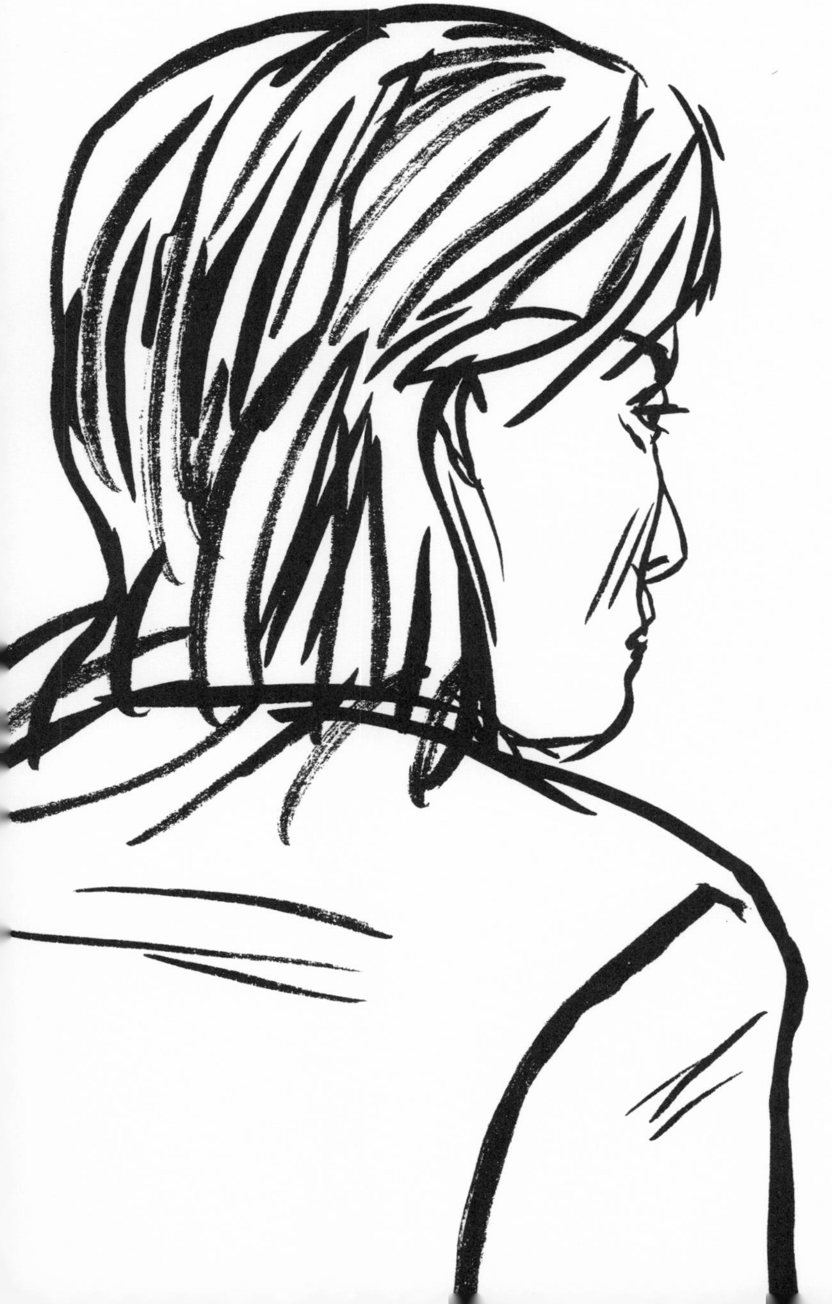

Margaret felt sick and was racked with guilt. But after reading about Scott's ex-girlfriends (and his difficulty in committing to them), what she felt was not exactly jealousy, fear, or suspicion: she felt love for Scott. Everything she adored about him was evident: the integrity he had toward his own instincts, his impatience with passivity, his boredom with shallow values, and his intolerance for cruelty.

This did not go far to alleviate her nausea, or slow the spool of images rushing through her head. But Scott's past, before she met him, was blameless, and real.

Louise ran into Greg's ex-girlfriend Lucy at a party and immediately developed a long, red rash on her neck. She left the party, but later that night experienced intense stomach pain. Louise rushed to the emergency room, but the doctors could find nothing wrong. She went home, but the cramps persisted, so she returned to the hospital. Again the doctors found nothing wrong. They sent her back home, where she curled up in a chair. By morning the pain had disappeared, as had the rash.